D0391299

RAISING READERS AND WRITERS

Raising Readers and Writers

A GUIDE FOR PARENTS AND CAREGIVERS

Robin
Knowing you has made
my life morelighthearted,
thoughtful, and comfortable!
Hugs always
Lenore

Carole S. Rhodes, PhD., and Lenore H. Ringler, PhD.

Raising Readers and Writers: A Guide for Parents and Caregivers

Copyright © 2021 by Carole S. Rhodes, PhD., and Lenore H. Ringler, PhD. All rights reserved. No part of this publication may be reproduced, stored in a retrieval system or transmitted in any form or by any means, electronic, mechanical, or photocopying without permission in writing from the publisher, except by reviewers, who may quote brief passages in a review.

ISBN 979-8-59-793233-0.

Subjects: Parenting, Literacy, Reading and Writing, Learning, Infancy through Middle School, Educational Development

The authors gratefully acknowledge permission to reproduce text and illustrations from *Ira Sleeps Over* by Bernard Waber. Copyright © 1972 Bernard Waber. Reprinted by permission of Houghton Mifflin Company. All rights reserved.

The authors gratefully acknowledge permission to reproduce text and illustrations from *Good Morning, Gorillas (Magic Tree House #26)* by Mary Pope Osborne and illustrated by Sal Murdocca. Copyright © 2002 Mary Pope Osborne and Sal Murdocca. Used by permission of Random House Children's Books, a division of Penguin Random House.

Reading is the key that opens doors to many good things in life. Reading shaped my dreams, and more reading helped me make my dreams come true.

–Ruth Bader Ginsberg

TABLE OF CONTENTS

Introduction

A group of kindergarten and first grade parents are sitting in the school library waiting for a parent workshop entitled "Reading and Writing: Helping Your School-Aged Child" to begin.

Steve:	I'm really interested in this topic. Marcy is just going into first grade, and I need to know what I can do at home.
Susan:	Me too. I did a lot of stuff with Pablo when he was younger, but now that he's in school full time, I'm not sure how much I need to do.
Leeann:	Well, I think that in today's world the more we do the better. All kids need "a leg up" if they're going to be successful.
Richie:	Yeah, but sometimes we try to do too much. Tom gets really annoyed when I ask him to read one of his stories to me.
Susan:	Pablo likes to read to me when it's a book he's picked out. I really hope this workshop gives me some new ideas about how I can help him to be a better reader and writer.

Raising readers and writers occurs within a family structure. Children become proficient readers and writers as they interact with parents, siblings, friends, and extended members of their family. What is the role of grandparents, aunts, uncles, and cousins as young children expand their literacy skills? The word *family* evokes many responses and for some of us has not just a personal meaning but a number of meanings. Have you ever heard of someone describe a good friend as a member of the family?

Traditionally family may have referred to two parents and one or more children living together. Today we see that modern families may occur in many different forms. In each of these families, children are learning to live together with adults and in many cases with other children. Regardless of the size of the family, in all of them listening, speaking, reading, and writing are the ways that children become literate adults and learn to function in our ever-changing world.

How and what children learn in their early years is critical to their future learning. Parents, grandparents, and caregivers all enhance children's learning in their early years, as well as when they enter formal schooling. These interractions profoundly affect children's future lives as readers and writers. It is up to you, and to all of us, to build the foundation that children need before they enter formal schooling. We play a vital role in children's learning, even of academic subjects such as science and history. As children progress from the early years of listening and speaking to becoming mature readers and writers, your role continues to be a vital one.

Some Background

As adults, when we listen attentively, we are generally putting together our thoughts while simultaneously forming a response to the speaker's words. This interaction, or conversation, between a listener and a speaker is how we communicate. An advantage of listening and speaking over reading and writing is that this means of communicating allows us to see the impact our words have on others. Speakers use facial expressions, gestures, and rising and falling tones as they speak. Speakers also notice their listeners' facial expressions and frequently respond to their questions.

Generally, speakers and listeners have a fairly easy time of understanding each other if they have some things in common. Think about the last time someone spoke to you about a topic with which you had no familiarity. A farmer would easily understand and talk about crop rotation, bioengineered food, and product distribution, but the average person might find these terms unfamiliar and conversation on these topics difficult to understand. And, of course, it is hard to understand someone who is speaking a language or dialect you don't understand or speak yourself.

In Figure 1 the speaker and listener have little overlap. That is, they have little in common, either about the topic being discussed or in the language being used. In a sense, they are talking at each other, not with each other. Because they share little in the way of ideas, their potential to learn from each other is limited. In contrast, in Figure 2, both speaker and listener are truly communicating and are sharing many ideas that may lead to new learning.

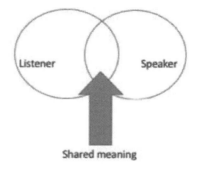

Figure 1

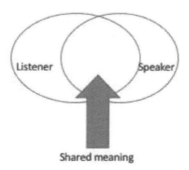

Figure 2

Here is an example of how this works. Greg, age nine, and his friend Heidi, age eight and a half, are planning a puppet show for school.

Greg: I think we should use hand puppets.

Heidi: I really wish we could use regular puppets, you know, the kind with strings and things.

Greg: So do I, but I think it would be too hard for us to make. If we use hand puppets, it will be easier, and we won't have to get help.

Heidi: You're right; the teacher said we have to do it ourselves.

Greg: Let's get some clean white socks.

Heidi: Okay, I'll ask my mother to take us to the store. What else will we need?

Greg: We'll need special markers, some felt, and some buttons.

Heidi: Maybe we should plan our script first, and then we'll figure out what our puppets will look like.

In this short conversation, it is clear that Greg and Heidi both have some knowledge of puppet shows and the teacher's requirements. They know that there are different types of puppets, and they also know and recognize their own limitations in creating puppets. It is also clear that they have a sense of the task they need to accomplish before embarking on this endeavor.

Children gain new understanding and knowledge when they share information, and parents, grandparents, and caregivers always need to keep in mind the two-way nature of a conversation. When adults converse with children, they should try to build on what the children know and should work to expand that knowledge. Parents are always observing their children and know the quizzical looks, blank expressions, and raised eyebrows that can indicate difficulty in understanding.

Things for you to think about as you and your child have a conversation include the following:

- What does my child already know about this topic?
- What new information does my child want or need?
- How can I add new information as part of the conversation?
- How can I find out whether my child understands the new information?

Here is a brief example that illustrates how a mother notices that her seven-year-old daughter, Sally, did not understand a word she used while they chatted during a shopping trip.

Mother:	We need to get an egg crate for Beth.
Sally:	I love to go shopping with you. Can I get to pick things out?
Mother:	I don't think there will be many things for you at this store.
Sally:	But the supermarket always has lots of things.
Mother:	We're not going to the supermarket, we're going to a bedding store.
Sally:	But only supermarkets sell eggs.
Mother:	Oh, I'm sorry, an egg crate is a foamy thing that people put on beds to make them feel softer. Beth needs one for her college bed.

As they grow, children listen and speak about many things with adults and other children. These experiences with listening and speaking help children learn about their world, and so the interactions need to be varied, frequent, and meaningful. Reading and writing build on the knowledge gained through listening and speaking. Reading and writing are ways of communicating, but they are obviously different from listening and speaking.

At those times when an individual is writing something for himself, the meaning of the writing should be completely clear. Take a shopping list, for example. If you have written the list yourself, you will understand it easily as you go up and down the store aisles, even if you haven't described all the items completely. For example, your written list may include the words *ice cream*. To you, this means a particular brand of ice cream, perhaps even a low-fat ice cream or frozen yogurt. But if you give the list to someone else, she may buy whatever appeals to her. On the other hand, if she knows you are dieting, she may be more likely to buy low-fat ice cream, though not necessarily the brand or flavor that you wanted. Very often, the context helps us to understand written materials..

To understand a writer, a reader needs to be on a similar wavelength. That is, the more the reader knows about the writer, the language that the writer uses, and the topic that is being written about, the easier it is for the reader to understand the written word. Look back at Figure 2 on page 3 and imagine substituting *writer* for *speaker* and *reader* for *listener*. The more overlap between the reader and the writer, the easier it is for the reader to understand the ideas of the writer. Areas of overlap include not only familiarity with the topic but also familiarity with the language the writer uses. All of this is a roundabout way of saying that new knowledge builds on previous knowledge, and new understanding builds on previous understanding. The way to foster this growth and development in knowledge and understanding gained through reading is by ensuring that our children have many experiences with a variety of books, magazines, newspapers, and other print materials.

Using This Book

As we planned the content of this book, we decided to focus on those literacy events that occur in families, often between parents and their children but frequently between members of the extended family and sometimes between children and a caregiver who is not a member of the family. While we tend to describe specific activities as involving an adult and one child, it is our intention that wherever possible these activities can be extended to include older and younger siblings. It is up to you to select those activities that are of the greatest interest to both you and your children.

For example, in chapter 5, the section "Going on Trips" provides detailed descriptions in which all members of the family can be involved in listening, speaking, reading, and writing experiences. These would include things like looking at maps to select the best route, choosing places to sleep over, and selecting places along the way that are of greatest interest to most of the family. These activities would lead to many conversations between the adults and children as they plan their trip.

In keeping with our perspective, in each chapter, we explore a number of questions for the developmental level that we are describing and suggest listening, speaking, reading, and writing activities for that level. It is crucial to always keep in mind that all children are different, even when they're the same age chronologically. Children vary not only in their physical growth but also in their language and learning development. We know it's natural to want to compare your child to some standard or to another child, but we suggest that you try not to do this. Just enjoy your child where she is and know that her growth will continue.

We have organized this book into seven chapters according to the usual developmental stages reached by children in particular age groups, starting with chapter 1, Your Infant, and concluding with chapter 7, Special Topics. But this in no way means that all children will neatly fit into the developmental levels we have described.

As you and your child begin this literacy journey, starting with infancy, we suggest that after reading this introduction, you scan the table of contents. Then read the first parts of the next few chapters, including the questions. By reading these brief sections, you will get a perspective of the whole book. At this point, as busy adults, you may want to select only the chapter that is most applicable to your child currently and read that in its entirety. Of course, we encourage you to read all the chapters because in each one there are ideas that can be modified for all developmental levels.

As reading and writing are the major foci of this book, it is understandable that in most of the suggested activities, children will read and/or write. Reading aloud is an activity that begins when your child is an infant and, for some of us, continues into adulthood as we read aloud to friends, family, and colleagues. Reading independently generally begins when a child becomes an "evolving" reader and continues throughout life. The process of listening to someone reading aloud and reading independently does not vary much. It is the content and the conversation that accompany each activity that change. Similarly, writing, which begins with scribble writing at an early age, becomes more complex as children mature and become adults. In some of the chapters, we give a great deal of detail about how children read and write and some illustrations. You may want to reread the pages noted below before you and your child engage in the many reading and writing activities that are suggested in other chapters:

Reading Aloud:	Chapter 3 pp. 46-51
	Chapter 4 pp. 76-82
Learning to Read:	Chapter 4 pp. 74-76
Reading Process:	Chapter 5 pp. 113-114
Encouraging Writing:	Chapter 4 pp. 84-87
	Chapter 6 pp. 138-142

While we describe many activities in this book, it is important to remember that these are only suggestions. Select those activities for which you have time, those you feel are most appropriate, and those that are of the greatest interest to you and your children. Perhaps the most important thing we would like to stress is that you should relax and enjoy your child. Laugh, play, talk, listen, observe, read aloud, read, and write together, and above all be sure that you and your children have fun learning.

There are four additional topics that we think are important and cut across several developmental levels. The first two concern the issues and policies involved in homework and standardized testing, both of which begin primarily in third grade and extend through secondary school. These two issues involve federal, state, and in some cases local policies and tend to be controversial. As a result, we will discuss some of the pros and cons of homework and standardized testing in chapter 7, Special Topics.

The third topic is using the computer for personal communication. We discuss using computers in ways appropriate to the developmental level of your child in several of the chapters. However, using FaceTime, Skype, Google Duo, and Zoom will also be discussed in chapter 7, as these platforms can be used as early as infancy, and their use will extend throughout your child's life. It is important to note that technology advances quickly, and you need to continue to monitor this area and adapt accordingly. The fourth special topic may be relevant if your child is having some difficulties with reading and writing and is the final one discussed in chapter 7.

We urge you to read this final chapter regardless of your child's developmental level and continue to be aware of how these special issues may directly impact your child's education.

CHAPTER 1

YOUR INFANT

Two fathers, Peter and Darryl are sitting at the playground with their young infants, who are sleeping peacefully in their strollers.

Peter: You know, my wife brought home one of those books made out of fabric for Jimmy, but he is only three months old! I sure don't know what she plans to do with that book.

Darryl: Oh, we have three or four of those little books in the house. I just bought a new one yesterday. Jamal loves them.

Peter: What do you mean he loves them? He doesn't really understand what you're saying when you read them, does he?

Darryl: Well, Jamal loves to sit with me or my wife while we read the words, and sometimes he seems to be looking at the pictures. The other day he even picked it up, and it seemed to me as if he was trying to open it.

Peter: Well, it seems like a waste of time for me to read books with Jimmy. Maybe when he's older.

Like Peter, many parents and caregivers do not see the point of reading aloud to very young infants. Darryl, on the other hand, seems to value the time he spends with his son as they look at a fabric book together. Although we agree with Peter that Jamal does not understand the words that his father reads to him, it is an important sharing time. It is critical to remember that infants are constantly learning, and it is the parents, grandparents, and caregivers around them who make this learning possible. Interacting with our young children, whether by reading aloud or talking about everyday things, provides important learning experiences.

In this chapter, we focus on the first year in the life of a child. This is a period of enormous growth, during which infants learn how to live with the objects and people they encounter. We describe what and how the young infant comes to know about this world, with specific focus on language. We also discuss activities for you to do with your child, including reading aloud, playing, and observing signs of language development. Through such activities, you help your infant learn more about his environment and about language.

Here are some questions to think about as you read this chapter:
- How does language develop?
- How does my infant learn about the world?
- What is so special about talking and playing with my infant?
- Why should I read to my infant?

Understanding the Infant

Crying can be considered the beginning of language, since it is the best way that an infant has of communicating his needs. When your infant cries, he may be telling you that he's hungry or just needs to be cuddled. Often, a child's parent and caregiver will begin to recognize different sorts of cries and their individual meanings. Crying because of a tummy ache can sound very different from crying because something is too hot or too cold. As you respond to your infant's communication, he begins to understand that he can make things happen and that you are dependable. Once your child passes the newborn stage, she will begin to experiment with ways of communicating in addition to crying. We have all heard infants babbling, which starts with making sounds and is common across many languages. Gradually, the infant begins to imitate those sounds that she hears most often. So, for example, a child growing up in a Chinese-speaking environment will soon stop making the sound *vee*, since that sound doesn't occur in the Chinese language.

At about six to ten months, a child's babbling begins to combine vowels and consonants. This may lead you to think that sounds like *mama* and *dada* are first words, but this is not necessarily true. It could be that your infant has merely stumbled on the babbled vowel-consonant combination to which you are assigning meaning. If you reinforce the child's communication with a response like, "Yes, that is your dada [or daddy]!" as you point to him, then she begins to learn more about language. By about eight months, infants also make sounds such as whining or grunting. These sounds, combined with babbling, crying, and gestures such as pointing, are an infant's way of communicating with you at this stage. You will certainly be able to understand your infant a good deal of the time, though the communication is not always clear, particularly to those adults who do not spend a lot of time with your child. We are sure that you are familiar with the scenario in which an infant's mother clearly understands what her infant wants but no one else does.

Around the age of eight months, infants also begin to understand the meaning of some words and phrases, although they are not yet able to speak themselves. If you play the game of "point to your eyes, point to your nose, point to your fingers, point to your toes" with your child, pointing to each body part as you say the words, he will soon be able to play along. You will be surprised at how the number of words your infant understands rapidly increases after twelve months.

Gradually, your child will move from understanding to speaking. The naming of objects is the beginning of spoken language. As you repeat the name of an object, your infant learns to link that sound or word with the object. For example, your infant may begin to say "ba" whenever he sees his bottle. If you respond by giving him his bottle, the sound *ba* will have a shared meaning for you, even though "ba" is not a real word. Soon your infant learns that every object, action, and so on has a name.

The words or vocabulary that your infant acquires may be quite different from the vocabulary of a friend's or neighbor's child. This happens because infants attend to words and phrases that are linked to what they are doing or thinking. Common first words include the names of important people, like *mama*, *dada*, and siblings' names. When your child hears you use words for different foods, body parts, pets, favorite toys, and actions such as "up" and "bye-bye," she begins to expand her vocabulary.

The Five Senses

Just as adults use their five senses to recognize and understand the environment and the people in it, so, too, do infants learn about their world through looking, listening, touching, smelling, and tasting. It is with their senses that infants begin to understand the people and events around them. Encourage siblings to interact with your new infant by showing her their toys while naming them as well as talking and reading short stories aloud.

Looking at the World
Everything that your infant looks at is new to him. He will respond to color, movement, shapes, and shades of light and dark. For the first two months, he will focus best on objects that are very close. That is about the distance your face is from him during feeding time. In fact, your face is one of the most important things that your infant sees frequently, and not only will he recognize you by it, but he will distinguish the different expressions that you make. By about three months, almost all infants can distinguish a parent's, grandparent's, and caregiver's face from that of a stranger's, and even very young infants know the difference between happy, sad, and surprised expressions on the face of an adult. Infants may even be capable of imitation. For example, if you pout, your infant may make a similar

face. Interestingly, if you hold your face still, it may appear to disturb your infant.

As parents, we all anticipate the day when our infant first expresses happiness with a smile. Before about twelve weeks, infants smile at things or people they see or hear without any differentiation. It is not until about three months or so that your infant will respond to you as you smile at him. This social smiling occurs when your infant's visual capacity has increased and he is able to focus his eyes on you and so respond to your smile.

Beginning at this stage of development, looking at objects becomes an important part of your infant's growth. Some infants as young as three or four months realize that hidden objects do not cease to exist just because they cannot see them. By about nine months, they are able to keep in mind the location of an object that has disappeared from sight and try to move so they can reach for it or grab it. Since the infant is interested in observing the world and the people in it, we need to provide objects for her to look at and create opportunities for her to interact with adults and older children in order to take advantage of her innate curiosity. For the young infant, toys in bright or strongly contrasting colors and in black and white, for example, are ideal. Remember to hold them close to your infant so it is easy for her to see them. Mobiles with objects in different colors and shapes, hung over the crib at a safe distance, are an excellent infant toy and one that can be easily made with cardboard, string, and crayons or paint.

Playing tracking games, in which you move an object slowly from side to side while talking to your infant about what you are doing, is a fun activity for her. Hiding a familiar object behind your back, for example, and then making it "reappear" takes advantage of your infant's growing abilities. Through these sorts of activities, your infant will begin to understand the objects around her. She will also be looking at the expressions on your face and learning to "read" them, an ongoing learning experience.

Hearing the World

Infants are very sensitive to sound. Newborns seem to react to sounds during their fetal period. Before birth, they hear their mother's heartbeat, a sound that remains very soothing to them in the days and weeks after birth. The unborn child at about twenty-four to twenty-six weeks of pregnancy can hear music, and it has been determined that classical music is particularly soothing to both the mother-to-be and her unborn baby. At about one month of age, infants connect sounds with their sources. Their favorite sound is the human voice, and your voice will probably be one of the first things to produce a smile. Even newborns seem to prefer their mother's or father's voice to the voice of someone else.

Young infants can distinguish changes in tone, loudness, length, and location of sounds. Since your infant is tuned into the sounds in his world, take advantage of this by talking to your baby often. Answer your infant's coos, smiles, and gurgles with sounds and words. Repeat the sounds that you hear your infant making. Other activities include singing lullabies, reciting simple nursery rhymes, and combining hearing and other senses in games like "peekaboo" and "pat-a-cake."

A simple talking and touching game begins with you asking, "Where is your foot?" Then touch your infant's foot and say, "There is your foot." Repeat this several times using different parts of the body.

Be sure to use types of sounds your infant likes best. Some infants prefer soft melodies, while others like music with a strong beat. And remember, if your infant turns away when you are talking or singing, he may be saying, "I want some quiet time now." Some infants naturally prefer a quiet environment, while others prefer a noisy one. It is best to follow the lead of your child, even an infant.

Touching the World

Infants use the sense of touch to explore objects around them. You can supplement this exploration by talking with your child as he investigates, naming the objects that he is touching, and describing their characteristics. Putting things in their mouths is one of the early forms of touching that infants use to recognize objects. The way an object feels in the mouth, rough or smooth, hard or soft, helps the infant learn about it. Some infants try to put everything they see or that you hand them in their mouths, while others may just look at objects or bang them. But remember to be safe and avoid choking by making sure that all objects around your infant are too big for him to put entirely in his mouth.

The more your infant grows, the more he is learning by using his hands to touch things that are nearby. Although infants can grasp things that are placed in their hands, they typically don't begin to reach for things until about three months of age. Offer your baby toys with lots of handles or other things that make holding easy. They should be light enough for your infant to lift and move around. By five or six months, infants can use their hands to examine objects more carefully. They may touch the surface to distinguish small details and move an object from hand to hand to determine size or shape. At about nine months, infants begin to distinguish between categories of objects. For example, they will begin to recognize the difference between objects that are round or square. Just as infants need to touch objects to learn about their world and to hear the words that identify them, so, too, do they need your touch. Stroking, cuddling, and holding her close are all ways of saying that you care.

Tasting and Smelling the World
Perhaps when we think about how our infants learn, we do not think of smelling and tasting as easily as we think about hearing, seeing, and touching, because these two senses prompt less of a reaction for us to observe. However, newborns do have a well-developed sense of smell. They not only are sensitive to odors in general, but they can tell one odor from another. Infants' sense of taste is also acute. Newborns differentiate sweet, sour, bitter, and salty flavors. When you introduce solid foods, you may notice your infant making

certain facial expressions in response to different tastes. Sweet tastes appear to have a particular calming effect. You can use your infant's developing senses and knowledge of language by making sure to attach words to different smells and tastes. How often have you said to your infant, "Does that taste good?" or "Isn't that nice and sweet?" We use language for the smells and tastes around us all the time. Even though you do not expect a verbal response from your infant, using words to express your thoughts is always a plus. Not only does your child begin the process of learning about language by listening to you, but the sound of your voice is a reward on its own.

Talking to Your Infant

We talk to our infants from the moment they are born. And why not? Talking evokes responses. As adults, we use language all the time to communicate with others. So why not use language to communicate with your infant? Infants will respond in their own ways. At one or two months, your infant will coo; by four months, she will probably begin to babble and reach out. By five months, infants seem to recognize the sound of their names.

Very often we use "baby talk" when we communicate with infants. We tend to raise the pitch of our voices, exaggerate intonation, speak in shorter sentences, repeat the sounds infants commonly use to name objects ("wawa" for water, for example), and pause longer between our utterances. Infants seem to know the tone of these communications, and they respond. However, if you feel silly or are uncomfortable using baby talk, then use actual words rather than repeating infant sounds. You may also want to repeat the infant sound followed by the actual word ("baba" followed by "bottle," for example). Whatever you decide to do, remember that the more you talk to your infant, the more responses you will get.

This two-way communication increases as your infant grows and reacts to the world around him. By eight months, infants start to indicate what they want by combining sounds like whining and grunting with gestures and looks in a certain direction. Sounds may be used to show emotion, such as crying, for example, from loneliness or boredom or to get attention. Between nine and eleven months, infants begin to imitate communication with adults by showing or giving them objects. If you are willing to engage in this form of communication, your infant will bring you many things, everything from toys to food to mud or lumps of dirt. By talking to your infant during this activity, you put words or labels to the objects that are familiar to her and help her begin to recognize and use language.

Before infants say their first words, they are able to understand the meaning of some individual words and phrases. It's always a delightful surprise the first time you say something to your infant that requires an action in response, and suddenly he does what you have suggested. Try saying, "Give me the teddy bear," or, "Put the doll in the corner," and watch for the response. The important characteristic of early communication is shared meaning of words as young children first talk about what they know.

Toward the end of the first year, your infant will probably discover the word *no*—and may begin to use it frequently! You need to be able to tell what your infant means when he says "no." Does he dislike something? If so, then it is important that you change the situation or the circumstance. Or is his seemingly defiant "no" a means of showing independence? Or has he just discovered the sound of "no" and repeats it without expecting any response from you? Sometimes young children's words have meanings different from the ones we usually understand. In some cases, it may be helpful simply to distract your child by engaging him with a favorite toy or word game. If you are patient and listen carefully, you will better understand your infant's communications, whether they are cries, coos, gestures, babbles, or first words.

Playing with Your Infant

Although infants do not begin to play with toys in ways adults might think of as conventional until about twelve months, there are many play opportunities for your infant before that age. In fact, playing with your infant will come naturally to you and won't need to be planned or organized. Tickling, dandling, or lightly bouncing her on your knee and having her touch parts of your face are all forms of play. Play can consist of you and your infant exchanging sounds, making faces, and observing responses; grabbing and holding fingers; looking at objects of different shapes and colors; moving objects around; and reaching out and grasping objects and dropping objects. Of course, for dropping objects to be considered play, you need to be there to pick them up! For your infant, the everyday things that you have in the house turn into toys. Pots and pans, measuring cups, and the television remote control can be favorite playthings.

Playing is also a learning opportunity for your infant, and games that involve the senses, particularly hearing and seeing, provide the best opportunities for learning about the world and learning about language. While having fun is the primary reason for playing with your infant, playtime involves talking to your infant too. As you and your infant interact, he is hearing new sounds, new words, and longer phrases and sentences and responding in his own way. This two-way communication during play is a natural, unplanned learning time.

Reading to Your Infant

Like Peter, one of the fathers in the scene at the beginning of this chapter, many parents think that reading to infants is a waste of time. Some even feel silly doing it. But we don't feel silly when we talk to very young infants, even when we know they don't understand what we're saying. Talking to your infant is natural, even though the conversation often feels one-sided! But, as we have pointed out throughout this chapter, even very young infants participate in communication and learn about their world and about language by listening to our talk, whether it be generated from conversation or by listening to a short story.

Sharing books with your infant cuddled in your lap is another way of being physically close, different from feeding time or comforting time. Your voice, which is familiar to him, comforts him in a new way. Reading to your infant combines seeing and hearing—and touching, if you begin with "touch and feel" books. Dorothy Kunhardt's *Pat the Bunny* is probably the best known of this type of book, but there are many others. These books include paper and objects with different textures for young children to explore with their sense of touch. The rhythm of the words as you read nursery rhymes or simple stories with repetitive phrases fills your infant's world with the sounds of our language.

There has been an explosion of publishing for very young children, so finding books to share won't be difficult. You will need only a few to get started because reading the same book over and over again will become part of the pleasure for both of you. As a parent, grandparent, or caregiver, you can observe how your infant reacts differently to the same book as he grows. Your infant, on the other hand, will benefit from hearing the same language, words, and phrases many times.

For infants, choose books with bright, colorful pictures, ideally one to a page. Cloth or board books with rigid cardboard pages are more durable than paper books, an important consideration, since you will probably read the same book many, many times. Avoid spiral bindings, since your infant may decide to chew on the book. Board books are a particularly good choice, as are fabric books, since you can throw them in the washing machine. Plastic books that float in the bathtub are another possibility for older infants. As you read aloud, try to vary your pace and change your voice for different characters in the story. Use whispers, tones of surprise or other emotions, and drawn-out vowels. This variety helps to keep your child focused on both your voice and the book. As your infant gets older, she will begin to mimic the sounds that she hears. Encourage this form of "playing" with the language. Make sure you are holding the book so your baby can see the pages clearly. Point to the pictures, and stop and talk about them. Encourage your infant to feel the book and to look at the illustrations.

You might also consider making your own books, with photos of siblings and other family members and objects that are familiar to your baby. Or you might decide to cut colorful pictures from magazines, mount them on plastic sheets, and write a word or short phrase on the page. A page with a snapshot of the family cat with the words "meow, meow" on it becomes something to talk about with your infant as you make the sound and both of you point to the cat's eyes, tail, ears, and so on. Pictures of other family pets, such as the dog, turtle, hamster, or fish in an aquarium, also make for lively conversations, even when they are mostly one-sided.

In this chapter, we have focused on talking, playing, and reading aloud with your infant. Activities that begin at this young age evolve through your child's early years and into the school years. While the toys, games, conversations, and books change dramatically over the years, the learning that occurs is continuous. Your child is listening to language, expanding her ability to use language, and beginning to understand how language functions in different situations. There is a special joy in reading aloud to a child and observing her responses. For some of us, listening to another person read aloud remains a very special event, as our language continues to grow and change right through adulthood.

CHAPTER 2
THE GROWING TODDLER

Two mothers, Frances and Beatriz, are sitting in a doctor's waiting room with their young children.

Frances: You know, Renee really surprised me the other day. Her stuffed rabbit fell under the table. I didn't think she could see it where it had fallen, but she walked right over and picked it up. So now we play a game where I tell her about things I've hidden, and she finds them. And you know what? She has started naming the things she finds!

Beatriz: Greg is also doing things I didn't expect. Last week he answered the telephone when it rang and said, "Hello," just the way I would. And he's not quite two years old! I guess he's been listening to me.

Frances: I guess a lot happens when they're toddlers, doesn't it? Sometimes I wish I knew what to expect. Then I could probably think up new things to do that would be fun.

Beatriz: I get lots of ideas right from Greg. After he answered the telephone, I bought him a toy phone, and now we have pretend conversations. He loves it! We really talk, you know. Not like a grown-up conversation, but he says things, and I say things back.

This conversation suggests how children at the toddler stage play, think, and learn and how adults and siblings can help in this growth. When Frances and Renee play the game of hiding and finding things, not only is Frances developing her child's ability to understand that objects, whether seen or not, remain the same, but she adds the important idea that objects have names by chatting with her daughter during the activity. Beatriz enhances her toddler's language growth in a different way by capitalizing on Greg's interest in the telephone. In both of these examples, the mothers took their lead from their children's actions.

This chapter focuses on the young child who is growing rapidly in her knowledge and understanding of the world and in her ability to communicate needs, ideas, and observations.

Think about these questions as you read this chapter:
- How does my toddler learn about the world?
- How do we as parents, grandparents, and caregivers help young children to learn language?
- What are some ways to make reading and writing fun activities for children?

Understanding the Toddler

Children at the toddler stage learn actively, through interaction with parents, siblings, caregivers, grandparents, and the world. They are immersed in language as the adults in their life feed, bathe, dress, listen to, talk to, and read to them. Your voice and the way you use language as you talk with your toddler will set a pattern for what is to come. At this toddler stage, they are constantly investigating and observing all aspects of their environment. Observing what your toddler does naturally and building on it is the gateway to making the early years a time of both play and learning. During these years, from about age one to about age three, children actively learn about their world through observation and mimic the talk of older children and adults around them, often taking delight in the silliness of some of the sounds they make. If you cook, she may begin to get out pots and pans, along with a spoon to stir with. If she sees you writing, she may pick up a crayon and imitate you. If you sing songs, she will likely start stringing sounds into melodies. As toddlers engage in a variety of experiences, they are expanding their listening and speaking vocabularies.

The one-year-old may be shy or nervous with strangers and may cry when mom or dad leaves. She may even show fear in some situations. Toddlers at this age do have favorite things and people. They may hand you a book when they want to hear a story or repeat sounds or actions to get your attention. They can even play games such as "pat-a-cake" and "peekaboo."

Toddlers at this age have developed physically to the point where they can get to a sitting position without help, stand by pulling themselves up, and may even take a few steps without holding on. Toddlers like to explore their world by shaking, banging, and throwing things. They can also find things you hide easily. One of their favorite activities is to put things in a container, take them out, and then do it again.

At this early stage of language development, your child may produce new words rather slowly, but his vocabulary will seem to explode after the first ten or fifteen words. From twelve to sixteen months, the vocabulary of the young child expands significantly. He will learn the names of many objects and will be able to identify them in pictures or in real examples. He will then begin to play with language. It is often difficult for adults to understand what a one- to two-year-old is saying and what he means by the words he uses.

While babies babble, toddlers near the age of two tend to "jabber," using sounds strung together as a means of communicating. Lindsay, a twenty-two-month-old we know, loves to add the sound of "-y" to the ends of words. She prances around the house, giggling while saying "book-y" or "ball-y." Her play with the sounds of language is an important part of the growth process. The jabbering often is melodic but incomprehensible. As language acquisition progresses, toddlers begin to point at and name objects. Children at this age also begin to connect names to the people they see most often. Parents or primary caregivers are usually named first, with siblings and grandparents following.

Toddlers at this age also begin to combine words into simple sentences containing verbs and nouns. Typical speech patterns at this stage include sentences such as "Go store" or "Grandma up." Here is an example of a toddler who is both observing his surroundings and using language to express his knowledge. Taylor, who is a little more than two years old, has often visited his father, a policeman, at his office. Now, whenever he passes any police station, Taylor says, "Daddy police." He has clearly been looking and listening during his visits to his father's workplace and has made a connection between his father, the office, and the work of police officers. At this stage, Taylor is dealing mostly with concrete ideas, but as he matures, he will move toward more abstract thinking.

Although you may be tempted to expand on your child's two-word utterances or correct your child's sentence construction, refrain from doing this. This is a time for children to experiment and play with language as much as possible in a risk-free environment, where their attempts are celebrated and applauded. It is important that communication between you and your child is always positive.

By age three, the toddler has grown considerably in his social, emotional, physical, and language development. He climbs well, runs easily, walks up and down stairs with one foot on each step, and is able to pedal a tricycle. He shows affection for friends without prompting, takes turns in games, and understands the idea of "mine," "his," or "hers." While a toddler at this age may get upset with major changes in routine, he is able to separate easily from mom and dad.

The concept of "time" is a difficult one for toddlers. They exist in the present and have no sense of time. Concepts like the past (yesterday) and the future (tomorrow) seem to be murky, even though at age three they may understand first or last and how long something takes (a long or short time). Children vary widely in how well they grasp time. Although toddlers can't tell time, it is notable how they develop a sense of order through repeated routines. One example is when you say, "We're leaving in ten minutes," they just know that they're not leaving now.

Whatever activities you and your toddler participate in, it is important to keep in mind his developmental level and his social and psychological needs. Be mindful of his interests and level of involvement. If he doesn't seem interested in a particular activity, discontinue it. Like all of us, your toddler has preferences, and it is wonderful to see this aspect of his personality emerging.

The World through Language

Providing rich experiences for toddlers does not need to be complicated, as even simple activities will help your child learn and grow at this stage. For example, when you and your toddler are playing with stacking toys or blocks, many concepts are developed.

Think about all the abstract ideas you introduce just through your natural conversation as you build a tower of blocks: This is an excellent time to include an older sibling whose language ability is more expansive than that of your toddler's. Just having your toddler listen to the ideas and vocabulary of his sibling is an important literacy experience for him.

- Color: "Let's put the yellow block here."
- Under: "Let's try the yellow one under the green one."
- On top of: "I put the red one on top of the green one, but it fell off."
- Next to: "Should we put this one next to the yellow one?"
- Big: "This one is too big."
- Small: "I found a small block to go here."
- Same: "Let's find a block that's the same size as this one."

The critical component here is that the abstract concepts are linked to concrete objects. As the child plays with the blocks, sees you moving them around, and hears language describing the action, her knowledge is expanded. The more your child observes and begins to understand the relationship between objects and words, the wider her base of experiences becomes, from which she can draw in the future.

There are numerous chances for even the busiest of parents to enhance the knowledge base and language experiences of their children. Look at and listen to things together and talk about what you see and hear. You might say, "I hear a bird. Do you hear the bird too? Maybe that singing means the bird is happy." Sing songs yourself, either to or with your child. Melodies are meaningful to children at this stage, and they love to hear simple songs like "London Bridge." They will begin to sing the songs themselves, replicating the melody and using their own sounds as they sing. Often these sounds have no relation to the actual words of the song, but this is still a language experience, and it will grow and develop into a more sophisticated form. When you go out for a walk, point out a dog, a store, or a flower you see. Simply by saying, "Look at the dog," you are helping your child make the connection between that four-legged animal and the word *dog*. If you can, take an older sibling with you and bring along a small tape recorder. As you walk, she can record the sounds you all hear as well as your conversations. You might hear a fire engine's siren, a bus horn, or a dog barking. When you get back home, play the tape and identify the sounds together.

On our very busy days, sometimes a quick story or rhyme while waiting in the supermarket checkout line is all we can do, but that is still an important contribution to your child's language experiences. Simple conversation can accompany a bath, a walk, a trip to the store, or simply relaxing at home. For example, during a bath, you can identify body parts as they are washed. Try playing "What's Next?" As you wash your child's arm, you might say, "What will we wash next? How about your hand?" In this way, you attach names to body parts. After a while, your growing toddler might take the lead and tell you which body part to wash next.

Through the excitement expressed by those significant adults around them, children gain confidence in their ability to communicate and will become more interested in language. Show your child how happy you are that she is talking with you. Enjoy the silliness of the words, phrases, and sentences, and realize that very soon they will develop into language that is understandable. Here are some suggestions for ensuring that your child is immersed in meaningful language throughout the day. These activities can be easily incorporated into even the busiest of schedules.

For the one- to two-year-old:
- Make up or recite silly little poems to your child when you change her diaper, give her a bath, feed her lunch, or play with her. This shows her that language is fun and can stimulate her sense of wonder and fascination about language and language-related activities.
- Help expand your child's vocabulary by playing "What's That?" Talk to him about things you see when you're out for a walk, running errands, or enjoying picture books together. By using language in these ways, you are stimulating curiosity, expanding vocabulary, showing concrete connections between words and things, and showing that language is an important form of communication.
- Sing songs. Songs are joyful expressions of language and often emphasize rhymes, which delight children.
- Play "Where Is It?" by hiding a toy under a blanket or behind your back and, through your conversation, encouraging your toddler to find and name it.
- Use language extensively when your child wants to play a familiar game: "Oh good, you brought me the ball. Let's roll it on the carpet."
- Respond when your child gives you nonverbal messages. Young toddlers often communicate by shaking their heads, pointing to things, or lifting their arms. Talk about what he

seems to want to tell you. For example, if your child points to something he seems to want, you might ask, "Do you want me to give you the ball?"

For the two- to three-year-old:
- Involve your child in routine tasks, like grocery shopping. Let your child write shopping lists with you, and talk to her as you clip and sort coupons. This can help your child learn some strategies for tasks such as classifying and categorizing that involve higher-level, abstract thinking.
- Make a "Question Bag." Hide a familiar object in a pillowcase or large bag. Give your child simple clues about what it is, its color or shape, how it can be used, and so on—and encourage him to guess what's in the bag. This gives him a chance to use language while developing deduction skills.
- Stick things on the refrigerator! Magnetic letters that you can use to spell familiar names and places (for example, your child's name, *mommy*, *daddy*, *zoo*) are useful. Use paste or double-sided tape to stick pictures of familiar things on magnets, and display these on the fridge. Talk with your child about these magnetic pictures. Display her artwork and ask her to tell you about it. Children have fun looking at pictures and saying the words that go with them.
- Make your own books to share. This can be as simple as stapling together interesting illustrated pages torn from magazines; putting your child's drawings, perhaps with captions you write, together in a binder or folder; or using an inexpensive photo album to create a photo essay of your family.

Some activities may be ongoing for several years. One father we know uses his mobile phone to take photos of his son, Khiem, at different times. Sometimes Khiem is alone, other times he is with his older brother or a friend. Khiem's father displays the photos in large format on a computer monitor and asks Khiem to tell him what he was doing in each shot. Khiem's dad then uses word processing software to type Khiem's own words on the screen as Khiem speaks, not only creating a caption for each photo but showing him quite literally how speech is connected to print. Each photo and caption is printed out to become one page in a permanent book. Khiem looks at this homemade book over and over again and loves to show it to his friends, siblings, grandparents, and caregivers. At some point he actually begins to "read" the words on the photo. Children love these homemade books whether simple or elaborate.

The World through Reading

Perhaps the most important thing you can do to prepare your child to become a reader and writer is to be a model for her. Research shows that children who are early and good readers come from homes where reading is valued and experienced regularly. Reading aloud to children shows them the joy that books bring, provides them with an example of what readers do when they read, introduces new vocabulary, and results in a strong bonding opportunity for both of you. It helps stimulate their imagination and offers opportunities to experience things that may not be readily accessible in their daily life. Additionally, when we read aloud with our children, they get to snuggle up close to us, so they feel loved and connect reading with pleasure.

As described in the previous chapter, listening to a book read aloud is a worthwhile and fun learning activity, beginning right from birth and continuing during the toddler years. Children at this age can look at the pictures, listen as we read, and point to various objects illustrated in books. As you read, point to the pictures and say the names of the objects. As your child gets older, you can connect the word to an illustration, as well as to an example of the real object. Beth, who was reading a book about getting dressed to her eighteen-month-old daughter, stopped to say, "Look! Here's a picture of a little girl combing her hair. She's holding a comb. Where's your comb?" Beth and her daughter then went into the bathroom to find her comb. "Yes, you've got a comb too!" Beth commented. "And I love to comb your hair." Beth introduced the abstract idea that pictures and words can connect to real things in a natural and meaningful way for her daughter.

Another way to make connections between objects and print is to point out written words in your child's world. You can point out signs at the park, at the zoo, or when you're out walking, shopping, or driving. When you visit the zoo and look at the lions, for example, point out the word *lion* on the sign displayed on the enclosure wall or fence. This will help your toddler connect the spoken word to the written word and to the actual animal. You might then look for a book about lions at the zoo shop or your local library. This is a good way to follow up your visit to the zoo by examining the pictures in the book and reading the text while pausing occasionally to talk about your zoo visit.

Similarly, when you are in the supermarket, your child is surrounded with labels that represent concrete, familiar objects. Make this into a learning experience by pointing familiar ones out to your child. Even young toddlers recognize the names and logos they see often on favorite foods. These activities reinforce the concept that we can both hear words and see them in print.

Parents often ask how to pick the best books for their children or for tips on the best way to read aloud. We're always happy to reply that there's no best book or correct way. It's the experience of being read to that is significant for the child. It doesn't matter if you read greeting cards, nursery rhymes, songs, cloth and tub books, or bright picture books. When you do use cardboard or cloth books, be aware that your toddler might enjoy looking at, tossing, or chewing the books more than being read to. The important thing is conveying the idea that printed materials can provide a pleasurable experience. At the end of a page or two, stop reading and ask your toddler to point at and name things. You might even keep old magazines and newspapers around the house and let your toddler play with them.

Sometimes a good book selection is suggested by an activity you might be planning. For example, if you're taking a short trip to a new place, you could find a picture book about that place, talk about the illustrations, and read it aloud both before and after your trip. Books can also be connected to familiar activities. Before you go to the playground, for example, you might want to read *Maisy Goes to the Playground* by Lucy Cousins. Afterward, you can remember your outing by reading the book again.

Make reading aloud part of your routine, not something for special occasions or to be used as a reward. Read as often as you and your child have time. If you don't have time to read a whole book, read just a bit. If your routine is too hectic to read every day, and this is true for many of us these days, then plan to read three or four times a week. Too many busy parents feel that they must read to their child every day, and then it becomes one more task rather than an experience that is relaxing and fun for all concerned. The important thing is to have a positive experience sharing language and time together.

It is helpful to set a good tone and mood before beginning to read aloud by giving your toddler and you time to settle down. For most children, reading stories aloud before bedtime makes a good transition between active play and rest time. One mother we know always stops reading at a very exciting or enjoyable point in the story so that she and her child will eagerly look forward to the next read-aloud. At this age, reading time is physical and social as well as intellectual. Children should be encouraged to talk, point, and follow along as they are read to. Let your child hold the book and turn the pages for you. Talk about the story and what's in the pictures. Be sure to read slowly enough so that your child understands the story. Try to read with expression and don't be afraid to ham it up! Also, be willing to stop reading if your child no longer seems interested. Above all, it is important to remember that reading to your child should be fun for both of you.

It is a good idea to take even the youngest child to visit the local library. One of Carole's fondest memories of her own early childhood years was when her mother, Fran, took her to the library. Watching her mother select books and seeing the enjoyment that Fran got out of the process told Carole, even at that very young age, that books led to pleasurable experiences. Take your toddler to the library so that she can choose books to listen to at home. Today many libraries are open in the evenings, so almost all parents can fit a library outing into their schedules and enjoy this activity with their children. Find out about your library's special books and services. Many libraries have special programs geared for toddlers. These programs generally encourage participation of parents and caregivers together with their children. They often open with a read-aloud, followed by activities such as storytelling, singing related songs or reciting rhymes, and finger plays.

Experiencing Writing

Many parents these days incorporate reading into their routines with their children, but most think less often about writing. However, writing development happens in similar ways to reading development as our children watch and learn from us. Also, reading and writing development are closely connected and reinforce each other. Think about how often your child sees you write at home. Most likely you write notes to yourself and others, shopping lists, checks, and phone messages. Your toddler probably also observes you as you sit at your computer and write emails, letters, greeting cards, or more extensive pieces such as reports for work.

The child of this age is often engaged in role-playing as she experiments with writing tools. She loves to scribble with markers, crayons, or pencils (on paper, we hope, rather than the walls). These early drawings and writing activities are the beginning experiences that will lead to more formal writing later on. They are your child's way of emulating your behavior, but they are also a basic form of communication for your child.

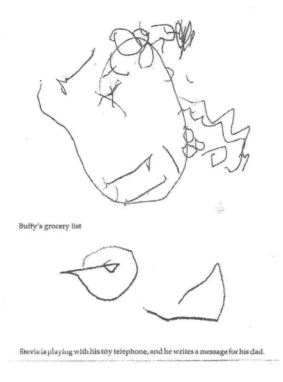

Buffy's grocery list

Stevie is playing with his toy telephone, and he writes a message for his dad.

FIGURE 3

It is very exciting when your child's scribbles begin to resemble real letters. To encourage writing, keep writing materials and different kinds of paper where your child can reach them. If possible, have a small desk or child-size table on which you can place these materials so that they are easily accessible to your child. Take books and writing materials for your children with you whenever you leave home so that they can read or write along the way or when you reach your destination. Talk to your child about his writing. Encourage him to read to you what he has written, as you probably won't be able to read it yourself, since he is very unlikely at this age to form correct letters or to have a sense of conventional spelling. Show your child how you read and write every day to have fun and to get things done.

There are many ways that we can begin to encourage writing as a form of communication. Share your writing with your child. As you write your grocery list, talk to your child about it. You may even assist your child in writing her own list. It can begin with talking about what she wants you to buy at the supermarket and move into cutting out a picture, which you label. Your child may simply put a mark on a page or scribble what she wants. Be sure to discuss this with her, and whenever possible, when you take your child to the market with you, be sure to buy what is on her list.

The Tools of Literacy

All children, no matter what their ages, need opportunities to explore reading and writing on their own. The everyday environment you provide in your home is critical here. To foster this independent learning, parents need to make sure the tools of literacy are available—drawing paper, writing paper, pads, crayons, colored markers, pencils, and books. Keeping these materials in a special place that is convenient for your child will encourage her to explore. Storybooks, especially ones you have read aloud to your child, as well as others you have not yet shared, need to be placed in an area that is relatively quiet and private, on shelves that are easy for your young child to reach or on a small table. As your child gets older, newspapers and magazines may be added, as well as a bookcase to hold all of her books, both those from school and personal books.

Another item that provides a great and easy way to show the many uses of reading and writing to your toddler is a large wall-hung calendar. Reminders about playdates, visits to grandparents or other relatives, doctor's appointments, and vacation times can be written by you on the appropriate dates. Then, together, you and your child can read and talk about what is happening on a particular day.

In these toddler years, as you play and learn with your child, it is important to keep in mind the developmental, social, and psychological aspects of your child. Be aware of your child's interests and level of involvement. If she doesn't seem interested in something, discontinue the activity. Don't worry that there's something wrong. We all have preferences, and it is wonderful, though sometimes frustrating, to see this aspect of personality emerging in our children. Encourage, support, and nurture your child's language activities, but most of all enjoy the time you spend together.

CHAPTER 3

YOUR PRESCHOOL CHILD

Two caregivers, Marie and Tamiko, are having coffee while the three children that they care for, ages three, three and a half, and four, are playing nearby in the next room.

Tamiko:	You know, I'm so glad you were able to come over today with Toni and Giovanna. Robert is a lot of fun to be with these days, but I'm getting so tired of answering all his questions. All he does is talk all day! I just say "yes" or "no" to most of his questions now.
Marie:	Well, I guess it's easier for me because Toni and Giovanna have each other to talk to. But sometimes they really want me to answer their questions. Just the other day Giovanna wanted to know why the sky was blue and why leaves were falling off the trees. I didn't know what to say, exactly, so we looked in a book she had about rain and clouds and the seasons.
Tamiko:	Well, that happens to me sometimes too. But when I just say "yes" or "no," Robert gets really angry and frustrated with me. It's like he wants more information, and sometimes I simply don't have all the answers!

Marie: Maybe you could try talking to him more about familiar things so he won't be so busy asking hard questions. I told Toni and Giovanna a story about when I was a little girl growing up in the country, and they had a lot of questions that I could answer. We had fun talking about how different my childhood was from theirs. And then they drew pictures of me in the country, and I drew a picture of them in the city.

Between the ages of three and five, children develop an almost insatiable curiosity. It is up to parents, grandparents, caregivers, and other adults to give them every opportunity to learn as much about the world as they can absorb. In this conversation, it is clear that Marie has figured out a way to engage Toni and Giovanna in conversations about things that she is familiar with and has information about. This is an excellent way for any adult to interact with children of this age. Focusing conversation on the child's interests and using stories and examples from your own life are ways to expand the child's knowledge, both of the world and of language.

By listening to what children say and by observing their reactions to a conversation, we can broaden their world and help them to make sense of it. By the same token, just answering by giving simple "yes" or "no" answers to a child who is seeking information may frustrate her and increase her need to ask even more questions. We need to remember that during these early years, children can easily absorb new ideas.

This chapter focuses on the critical years before a child goes to school. These are the years in which parents, caregivers, and other adults provide many opportunities for literacy learning. They use "teachable moments," those natural opportunities for helping a child gain new knowledge and understanding. As children listen and talk and respond to their world in writing, drawing, or play, they are organizing their thoughts and communicating them to others.

Children also expand their understanding of the many forms of communication when they see you doing your own reading and writing. It is up to us to give them every opportunity to learn as much about the world as they can. Here are some questions to think about as you read this chapter:

- What are some of the ways that my young child's use of language expands?
- How can I provide those opportunities that will help my child become a reader and a writer?
- What are some techniques for reading aloud to my preschooler?
- What learning activities can we regularly do together?

Language Development

As your child grows, so does their ability to use language. Children are naturally active, and this is true of their language learning too. They learn about language as they use language and hear it used in varied different situations. Researchers believe that language and thinking begin to intermingle at about two years of age, so that children start to use language in their minds as they think about things. At this stage, the child also begins to share ideas and expand them by listening to the language of others. In this way, language becomes intellectual and thought becomes verbal. Children use language to explore relationships with people and things in their environment. Between two and three, children begin to take the listener into account, making their communication more interactive as they learn to say things in a way that makes the meaning clear to their audience. This skill develops slowly until age seven or eight.

Children as young as four have been observed to change their speech when they are talking to younger children. They use shorter sentences, speak more slowly, and use simpler words to make it easier for the younger child to understand them. Just as the preschooler adjusts his speech for the toddler, parents, grandparents, and caregivers need to keep their children's developmental stage in mind in conversations with them.

The five-year-old knows colors and draws pictures that represent people, objects, and animals. By age five, children understand that stories have a beginning, a middle, and an end and that books are to be read from left to right and top to bottom. Children of this age like to experiment, make their own decisions, and often take risks. Even children as young as four will sometimes simply need to get away and be by themselves.

Children of this age tend to do the following:
- Ask questions
- Store information about the way language is used
- Increase their vocabulary
- Expand their understanding of concepts

During this preschool period, language gradually becomes freed from the immediate, concrete environment, and the child begins to use his language to think about and express ideas about people, objects, and events even when they are not present at the moment. As a result, the child's memory store expands. Growth can be seen in the ability to rely on past experiences and in the language used to identify and categorize new objects and events.

Listen, for example, to what is revealed about a four-year-old's understanding of the difficult concept of death in this conversation between a mother, Birgit, and her son, Adam. It's the US Presidents' Day holiday, and the two are at home together.

Adam: Why are you home today?
Birgit: Well, it's Presidents' Day. That's a holiday when we remember some of the great presidents. Your school is closed, and I'm not working so I can be home with you.
Adam: Can we watch the great presidents on TV?

Birgit:	No, I'm afraid not. These presidents died a long time ago.
Adam:	Did they throw the presidents in the garbage?
Birgit:	No, why do you think people would do that?
Adam:	I remember you saying the flowers were dead, and then I saw you throw them in the garbage.
Birgit:	Well, you're right about the flowers. I do throw them in the garbage when they are dead. But it's different with people.
Adam:	How is it different?
Birgit:	Well, when people die, we have special ways to say goodbye to them.

This conversation illustrates not only Adam's understanding of the word *dead* but also how an adult can expand a child's knowledge by providing information and responding to questions without adding information that is beyond the understanding of a four-year-old.

Everyday life presents many opportunities for parents and other adults to enrich young children's language development and their understanding of the world around them. Children learn about language and literacy in many ways. They see that print is everywhere in their world; they take part in day-to-day conversations; they ask questions; they observe adults and older siblings reading and writing. As adults, we can provide an environment that is rich in print, create an atmosphere in which asking questions is encouraged, and take advantage of "teachable moments" to enhance their understanding.

Eating together, watching television, and playing together are activities that occur frequently and naturally in most families and are perfect opportunities for conversations that will enrich your child's language abilities. It is also important to plan special activities that are of interest to both you and your child and fit in with your family life. These activities do not need to be complicated, and many require minimal planning. The local zoo, the children's section of the library, or a food market are excellent places to visit. Other activities, such as reading aloud, storytelling, cooking together, and playing games, require more planning. These activities and others are described in the remainder of this chapter.

Almost all children enjoy outings, and preschoolers are no exception. Four- to five-year-olds are constantly observing their environment, trying to make sense of it and express their thoughts through language. Neighborhood walks, going to the playground, shopping, and visiting friends and family are all perfect opportunities for conversations that will expand children's language abilities. As children get older, they can become involved in the many planning activities that are a part of family vacation times. We have described many of these activities in chapter 5, in the section entitled "Going on Trips" (pp.120-123). As you skim this section, you may find some activities that you can adapt for your preschool child.

Reading Aloud

Just as it was when your child was a toddler, time spent reading aloud to your preschooler can be a very pleasant experience. To make reading aloud fun for both you and your child, make sure you have nothing else on your mind before beginning to read and that you are engaged in the activity. If you are preoccupied, reading aloud may seem like a chore, and your child will sense your feeling.

Although most of us have heard about how important it is for parents to read to young children, there is more to it than just reading. The critical part of reading aloud to your child is the conversation that takes place before the reading, during the reading, and after the story is completed. This conversation is what makes reading aloud both a pleasant experience and a learning experience.

Let's listen in as Mitch reads *Ira Sleeps Over* by Bernard Waber to his four-year-old daughter, Sarah.

Note: When Mitch is reading to Sarah "she" refers to Ira's sister.

Mitch (before showing Sarah the book):

        Remember last week when you went to Nicole's house for a sleepover, and you took your fuzzy cat with you?

Sarah: I like Pom-Pom to go everywhere with me. I get to talk to her.

Mitch: Does Nicole have an animal that she sleeps with?

Sarah: No. She has a funny blanket that's all messy-looking, and she takes it to bed.

Mitch: Well, when I was at the library last night, I went over to the children's section to find something new to read to you. I got talking with the librarian a bit, and he thought you might like this one.

Mitch shows Sarah the book cover.

Mitch: It's about a boy named Ira who goes on a sleepover. I guess that's Ira on the cover.

Sarah: Looks like he's got a fuzzy animal. A teddy bear, I think.

Mitch: Do you think he'll take the bear to his friend's house?

Sarah: I guess.

Mitch: Well, let's read some of the story and see if Ira takes his bear to his friend's house. The name of the story is *Ira Sleeps Over.*

Mitch (reading): I was invited to sleep at Reggie's house. Was I happy! I had never slept at a friend's house before. But I had a problem. It began when my sister said, "Are you taking your teddy bear along?"

        "Taking my teddy bear along!" I said, "To my friend's house? Are you kidding? That's the silliest thing I ever heard! Of course, I'm not taking my teddy bear."

Mitch: Sounds like Ira may have a problem. Do you know what a problem is?

Sarah: It's like when you don't know what to do.
Mitch: That's right. I wonder what Ira's problem is.
Sarah: I dunno.
Mitch: OK, let's see if we find out when we read more.
Mitch (reading): And then she said, "But you never slept without your teddy bear before. How will you feel sleeping without your teddy bear for the very first time? Hmmmmmmmm?"
Mitch: Oh oh. I can imagine how you'd feel without Pom-Pom!
Sarah: Yeah. I'd be really sad. I bet Ira will be sad too.
Mitch: I think so too. Let's turn the page and see.
Sarah (pointing to the cat): Look, Ira has a real cat—mine's only a toy cat. Why can't we have a real cat?
Mitch: Maybe when you're older.
Sarah: And I'll take care of it.
Mitch (reading): "I'll feel fine. I'll feel great. I will probably love sleeping without my teddy bear. Just don't worry about it," I said.
           "Who's worried?" said she.
Mitch: Well, Sarah, I guess we were wrong about Ira feeling unhappy.
Sarah: I would be sad without my Pom-Pom.
Mitch: Maybe Ira will change his mind.
Mitch (reading): But now, she had me thinking about it. Now, she really had me thinking about it. I began to wonder. Suppose I won't like sleeping without my teddy bear. Suppose I just hate sleeping without my teddy bear. Should I take him?

Sarah: I think he should take him.
Mitch: Why do you think he should take his teddy bear?
Sarah: 'Cause I take my cat when I go to Nicole's house to
             sleep.
Mitch (reading):   "Take him," said my mother.
                   "Take him," said my father.
                   "But Reggie will laugh," I said. "He'll say I'm a baby."
                   "He won't laugh," said my mother.
                   "He won't laugh," said my father.
                   "He'll laugh," said my sister.
                   I decided not to take my teddy bear.
Mitch: Do you think Ira will miss his teddy bear?
Sarah: Mmmmm.
Mitch: Now I think we know Ira's problem.
Sarah: He doesn't know if he should take his teddy bear or
             if he shouldn't take it.

Mitch: You're right. And it looks in this picture like he's still not sure.

This excerpt of a conversation between a parent and a child demonstrates several techniques you can use with children of this age to add to the pleasure of reading aloud. These techniques are useful regardless of what you have chosen to read and include the following:

- Ask a question and have a brief conversation before beginning to read. The question should focus the child's attention on the story and get him ready to listen attentively. Ask him to predict what the story will be about, or use Mitch's approach and ask something that will relate the story to the child's previous experience.
- Stop reading to answer your child's questions.
- Stop reading at critical points to either clarify or elaborate on something in the story.
- Stop reading to talk about a character and how that character in the story makes you and your child feel.
- Stop reading to ask a question about the story and what may happen next. Then read on to see if the prediction was accurate.
- Stop just before the end of the story or chapter and ask your child how the story might end.

When you finish reading the book, the conversation may focus on one or more aspects of the story. Any of the following questions can spark an engaging discussion with your child. Remember that these questions are supposed to begin a conversation in which you participate as well. Be ready with your own answers and your comments and reflections on your child's point of view.

- Did you like the story? Why?

- Was there a character you especially liked? What about one you thought was mean, or scary, or that you just didn't like at all?
- Was there a part of the story that you especially liked or disliked? (You may choose to reread that part.)
- Did the story end the way you thought it would?
- Did you like the ending? Why?
- If you wrote this story, would you give it a different ending?

If you have time and your child is interested, you can encourage him to draw a picture, write some comments, or act out parts of the story with some members of the family. Reading aloud has advantages other than the obvious ones of helping children expand language and extend knowledge. As your child observes your reading, he is internalizing many of the conventions of book reading and print. As he shares more and more read-aloud times with you and as you point out that books have special covers, that the title of the story is on the cover and on the inside page, that the name of the person who wrote the story is also on the cover and the inside page, that the pages are turned in order, and that the print is read from left to right, he will begin to understand more about books.

While we may not talk explicitly about book and print conventions with children of this age, they tend to be keen observers and may have questions for you. As in other situations, answer his questions at the level that you think he can understand. For example, if your child notices the date 1998 on the copyright page and wants to know why it's printed there, you could simply tell him that that is the year that the story was written.

Whether your child is four or five, reading aloud to her will be a similar experience throughout this preschool stage. It is a private time between an adult and a child, a time that is planned and uninterrupted by others. The place selected for reading may be a quiet corner of a room, the floor, the bed, or an especially comfortable chair. It's a time for sitting close together, sharing an experience, and enjoying each other. Some parents prefer reading aloud just before bedtime, but this is a personal choice. We know some parents who, when they read aloud just before their child's bedtime, tend to fall asleep before the child!

Perhaps the one difference in reading aloud as your child moves through the preschool years will be the choice of books to share. Attention spans begin to lengthen, though they are still quite short during this time, and you may move from simple picture books to longer stories. Choosing the right book to read to your child can be a part of the experience. Very frequently your child will know exactly what book she would like you to read aloud. Often it is a book that she knows very well and has heard many times. This repeated reading of familiar books creates an atmosphere of confidence. She knows what will happen next, and she may even decide to "read" along with you. The local library, your child's teacher, and friends are all good sources of recommendations for read-aloud books. Some recommended books for various age ranges can easily be found on the internet.

Storytelling and Nursery Rhymes

Storytelling is often a very personal activity, in which you make up a story about characters that your child is familiar with. These stories can be about the child, a friend, a member of the family, or yourself. Your child may be very interested in hearing stories about your own childhood, particularly what happened to you when you were the same age as your child is now. You may also have stories that have been told in your family for generations. Of course, these are wonderful to share and for maintaining family traditions. Furthermore, you may enjoy making up stories full of fantasy and adventure. Each type of story for storytelling is more than acceptable, and together they provide you with a variety of possibilities for the storytelling time you set aside.

Stories that you tell should be very much like the stories you read aloud. They should be fairly short and with a clear beginning, middle, and end. Just as when you read aloud, this is a private time between you and your child and should not be interrupted. It can be useful to connect the story to something in your child's own life. Here is a story told by a mother to her four-year-old daughter a few days before they were going on a trip to visit the girl's grandmother:

> A long time ago, when I was four years old, my mother told me that we were going to visit my grandmother. My mother said, "Grandma lives very far away, and we will be going on an airplane. It will take us two hours to get there." The next day we took a bus to the airport and waited on a line to get our tickets and boarding passes so we could get on the right airplane. We gave the tickets to the man at the gate and found our seats in the airplane. I got a seat next to the window. After we were up in the air, a man brought us something to eat and some crayons and paper for me. I made a picture of the airplane, and then it was time to land. As soon as we got off the airplane, I could see my grandma waving at us. My mother and I stayed with Grandma for a whole week. We played a lot of games and had fun. Then we took an airplane back home.

This short story has the same structure as a written story (beginning, middle, and end), relates to a family member, and is about an experience the child is about to have. Stories of personal experiences are fairly simple to make up, can be told almost anywhere, and tend to be short. Telling stories like this encourages your child to make up stories about people and things that he is familiar with. For many children, this sort of storytelling is a first step to writing stories.

Reading or reciting nursery rhymes aloud is different from reading a story aloud. Nursery rhymes emphasize the sounds of words, have a particular rhythm, and are very compact. They contain phrases to chant, silly made-up words that children love to mimic, and repetitive phrases. By sharing nursery rhymes, we help children recognize the patterns and sounds of language. They encourage us to make songs from some of the words or phrases, or to adapt some of the silly words to our everyday lives. By encouraging this sort of word play, we promote a love of language. And, as with favorite storybooks, reading the same nursery rhyme again and again shows children the relationship between sounds and the letters representing them. This is an important step in learning to read. In selecting rhymes to share, it is important to find those that have rich language and rhythm. When you select a book of nursery rhymes to read aloud, make sure there are illustrations that will help your child form visual images.

Drawing and Writing

Drawing and writing are activities that children can do by themselves or with you. If she works alone, she will develop the ability to enjoy private time and become more self-reliant, and she will provide you with some private time of your own. Drawing and writing can occur spontaneously if you make sure that paper, crayons, markers, and other tools are available, or they can be specifically planned as opportunities for language development. Generally, for children of this age, drawing and writing activities are best planned to follow some special event. For example, after a trip to the zoo, you might encourage your child to draw a picture or write something about the animals that he saw so that he can share something about the trip with someone in the family who was not able to come along. Other events that could lead to drawing and writing include birthday parties, visits to friends and relatives, and going to the movies or watching television.

Children draw pictures of their family, friends, pets, house, apartment, or neighborhood and other things that are familiar to them. Each of these drawings can spark a conversation. Many times preschool writers add scribbles to their drawings. While these scribbles may not resemble your writing, they are real communication. Actually, we call it "scribble writing," and it is the important first step toward more conventional writing. You may not be able to read it, but usually your child will be able to "read" it to you. Children are generally pleased to read their message to an adult. All you need to do is ask! As children develop in their ability to write, their messages become longer and more complex. Even mature readers need an audience, so be prepared to read his work and to react positively.

Starting a family log of special events provides many opportunities for drawing, reading, and writing. This log, which can be kept in a large notebook, needs to be something that everyone in the family contributes to. For example, if you have just returned from a business trip, you need to write something in the family log about it. It can be as simple as the date and one or two sentences. "Friday, December 18, 2020. I liked New York, but I'm really glad to be home!"

For a three-, four-, or five-year-old, the family log is a special place to share a special event by writing or drawing something that someone else will read.

This is an example of a four-year-old's log entry. When asked to tell about what he wrote, Ben said, "This is Daddy and me. Every day Daddy and me go to the store." In telling his story about a trip to the supermarket, he described the man at the checkout counter and some of the items they bought. The family log becomes a record of everyone's special activities and can be read and reread many times.

More Language Opportunities

Playing Together
The most important part of playing with your child is to follow his lead in deciding what to play and then engage in the playtime enthusiastically. Children of all ages are aware of their parents' and caregivers' level of response, interest, and feelings. Are you bored? Are you waiting to do something that you feel is more important? Are you tired? Are you feeling overworked and out of sorts? If the answer to any of these questions is yes, then it is not a good time to play with your child. But when the answer to these questions is no, it's time to put things aside and play. Also, hopefully you will not answer the telephone while playing with your child, unless you are expecting an important call. When you are ready to play with your child, it becomes a positive experience and one in which your child's knowledge and language can be expanded.

Doing a jigsaw puzzle may involve several children of different ages. No matter whether you are working on a simple twenty-five-piece puzzle with young children or doing a seventy-five-piece puzzle with older children, the language that you use demonstrates difficult or abstract concepts. As your child works on the puzzle, you are able to observe whether or not she understood the concept by her actions.

Here are some concepts that evolve as a jigsaw puzzle is put together:
- Over: "Let's turn all the pieces over so we can see them."
- Next to: "That piece looks like it fits next to the blue one."

- Top: "That piece fits at the top of our puzzle."
- Bottom: "Try that yellow piece at the bottom of the puzzle."
- Together: "Look, those two pieces are stuck together."
- Turn around: "Try to turn that piece around."
- Under: "Let's try the yellow piece under the green piece."

Jigsaw puzzles are usually very colorful, and so they provide many opportunities for talking about different colors and shapes as the pieces are fitted together. With older children, number concepts can also be included as you discuss the number of pieces still to be fitted to complete the picture.

Involving more than one of your children in board games and simple card games provides many additional opportunities to increase language and understand important concepts. Rolling the dice in a board game is a chance to expand number concepts. For example, first the player needs to count the number of dots on the dice, and then he needs to make the correct number of moves on the board. As the child's understanding of numbers progresses, she can add numbers when two or more dice are used.

Other concepts involved in board games include the following:

- Same: "We are in the same space."
- Ahead: "How many spaces ahead of me are you?" "It's your turn to move ahead of me."
- Behind: "I'm four spaces behind you."
- Turn: "Whose turn is it now?" and/or "Turn the next card over." (Note the two different meanings for *turn*.)
- Forward: "You got a four, so you can go forward four spaces."
- Backward: "Your card says you need to go backward three spaces."

Card games can develop some of the same concepts. For example, in Go Fish, we frequently use *same*, *different*, *turn*, and *ahead*. In the card game War, the concepts of *higher*, *lower*, and *matching* are critical.

Many children of this age also enjoy dramatic play and use make-believe and dress-up types of activities. This type of play encourages creativity and imagination. The materials needed for dramatic play are the everyday clothes, hats, scarves, and shoes that you may be discarding. Children enjoy dressing up and then making up a "play" or "stories" to go with their costumes. Language is the tool they use to tell their stories. Since language development depends on communication between two or more individuals, you, the audience, are a crucial component of this play activity. Remember to be an attentive audience for their performances. How you react, what questions you ask, and how involved you seem to be are all understood by your child.

Simple outdoor activities such as throwing a ball back and forth lend themselves to many opportunities to expand language. In playing games of any kind, it is important to remember that conversation is a part of the game. Here are some concepts that may be developed as you and your child toss a ball:

- Close: "You are standing a little too close to me."
- Back: "Move back a little bit."
- Closer: "Come a little closer to me."
- Together: "I like the way you keep your hands together to catch the ball."
- Apart: "See how my legs are apart. Can you try that?"
- Near: "Wow! That ball came very near to my head."
- Far: "I really threw that ball far away from you."

Shopping Together
Shopping with a young child can be an exhausting experience, but with a little bit of planning, going shopping with your young child can turn from an exhausting undertaking into a fun experience that's also rich in language learning. Including another family member in a shopping expedition may be helpful, but you are the best judge of how well this works. One thing to remember is that your child has a limited attention span, and so a shopping expedition needs

to be relatively short. Part of the experience is the planning you do together before going to the store. Make a shopping list together, for example. Your child can dictate some of the items you need to buy while you write them down. This activity helps children associate the spoken word with the written word. They may begin to notice that certain letters represent certain sounds as you write down their words. For this to happen, you will need to use clear printing and complete words, not the shorthand sort of list most of us routinely prepare.

If you are going grocery shopping, you might group the items that go together, such as fruits and vegetables, dairy items, and so on. Ask your child questions, such as, "When we buy apples, is there some other fruit that we can buy too?" You could even encourage your child to help you put the items in categories by using his knowledge of the store. Making a simple map together of how the store is laid out is one idea. Once this map is made, you can use it to organize your shopping list in the order of the aisles where the items are found. During the actual shopping expedition, your child can locate items by comparing the words on the package with the words on your list if you have written them in large print. Putting groceries away when you come home is another opportunity for categorizing. Think aloud as you put things away. "Let's put all the things that go in the freezer away first. Now give me all the cold things that go in the refrigerator. I'll put the canned juice and soda in the cabinet. The cookies fit on this shelf."

Opening the Mail

For many of us, opening the mail is a daily activity that we do as quickly as possible each day. If you are willing to spend a few extra minutes, however, this task can be turned into a learning activity. Sorting the mail into categories (perhaps magazines, catalogs, bills, junk mail, personal letters, and so on) with your child is one simple activity. The categories should be whatever is most helpful to you. Go through the piles with your child and ask her how she might decide where to put a piece of mail. When the sorting is done, ask your child which pile she would open first, and show her which pile you would pick. Discuss your choices and why you made them. You may also let your child pick a piece of mail that looks interesting to her and ask why she chose that piece. Ask questions such as, "What made it look interesting? What do you think might be inside?" If the piece of mail selected requires a response, you might at a later time involve your child when you work on your response. Thinking aloud about what mail you will keep and what mail you will throw away helps your child to see the difference between important and unimportant mail and how you make such judgments. While this is a fairly simple activity, it promotes a number of skills. These include understanding that written language is a way to communicate with others, associating print with spoken language, classification, following directions, and establishing priorities.

Planning a Party
Is a three-year-old too young to be involved in planning his birthday party? He will probably have lots of good ideas, even though some of them may not be very practical. Just think of all the possibilities for language learning that party planning involves. First, you'll need to make a list of friends and family to invite. As your child thinks of the names of the people he wants to come, he will see you write down each one. He can then help you write out the actual invitations, perhaps adding a drawing, or for the older child, printing some of the letters, or maybe just sticking the stamps on the envelopes. Depending on the age of the child, this is another opportunity for him to associate the spoken word with the appropriate written symbols. Some children of this age already know some of the letters of the alphabet. So when you write *Jane* and then later on write *Jamal*, your child may say that both names begin with the same letter, or with *J*.

Next comes a list of party food and supplies. This, of course, becomes an opportunity to shop together for food, games to play, and party favors to give the guests. Then, on the day of the party, you might write out each guest's name on tags that your child can give to his friends as they come in. Finally, reading birthday cards together and writing thank-you notes provide additional chances for expanding language. As you write thank-you notes, your child may only contribute a scribble or one letter to stand for his guest's name, but that is a critical part of the activity. You may also consider having your child make thank-you cards, rather than using store-bought ones, by taking some of his drawings and cutting them into card-size pieces.

Cooking Together

It's often difficult to find time to cook together as a family, but an occasional cooking session can be fun and is worth planning for. Select something simple to make that involves only a few ingredients and can be completed in less than half an hour. Baking cookies and making puddings lend themselves to this kind of shared activity. Using a packaged mix is probably the easiest, but here is a recipe that is simple and appealing to children.

Coconut Macaroons

Preheat oven to 325°F.
1. Cover cookie sheets with well-greased aluminum foil.
2. Stir together until well-blended 2/3 cup sweetened condensed milk, 1 large egg white, 1½ teaspoons vanilla, and 1/8 teaspoon salt.
3. Stir in 3½ cups flaked or shredded coconut.
4. Drop dough (about a tablespoonful at a time) onto cookie sheets.
5. Bake until brown (about 20-25 minutes).
6. Let stand until cool, and then peel the cookies from the foil by hand or with a spatula.

Package directions or recipes can be read aloud in their entirety to begin with and then read step-by-step as you follow each item.

The conversation that you have with your child about the ingredients and the steps for making cookies or pudding is an integral part of this activity. Not only does the conversation support your child's growing understanding of communication, but your child will become aware of the importance of following directions and of the fact that directions have to be followed in sequence. So, in the above recipe, coconut is the last ingredient. Here are some concepts that can be expanded as you and your child cook together:

- First: "What shall we do first?"
- Next: "I'll put butter on the cookie sheets next."
- After: "What do we do after the cookies are brown?"
- Before: "We need to stir everything together before we put in the coconut."
- Last: "What is the last thing we need to do?"

Going to the Library

For some people, going to the library means dusty books, librarians telling them to be quiet, and people trying to study. While libraries may have been like that at one time, they aren't anymore! Today's libraries have computers, videos, games, and puzzles to borrow, in addition to the usual books, newspapers, and magazines. Libraries today are lively, active places and often have special children's areas designed to be interesting to preschoolers and emergent readers. Librarians also frequently arrange events such as movies and special story hours.

Many libraries will let you get a library card in your child's name, even when she's very young. When she's old enough, she might like to get a new one and print her name on it herself. Having a library card makes your child a member of the library and connects her to the reading community. In addition to going to the library for special activities, one of the best ways to get your child involved in the library is to let her explore books in the children's section. Just looking through books independently is a great activity. If one or two books seem to have special appeal, you can borrow them to read aloud to your child. Showing your child some of your favorite books from your own childhood is another way to interest her in books and reading. Try to follow her lead, and just because you liked the book doesn't mean she will.

Using Media

Television and computers are now a part of everyday life, even for young children. While the media is always there and therefore easily available, it is you, the adult, who needs to be in charge. Given this widespread availability, parents, grandparents, and caregivers need to take an active role in guiding young children's media use.

Television

Most preschool children watch television, but what they watch and how often they watch needs to be up to you. Although many parents are rightfully wary of television programming, in the last several years, government intervention has brought some improvement in issues of quality and appropriateness. Television stations are now required to broadcast a minimum of three hours of educational programming weekly. Programs must be labeled, and shows are rated by age appropriateness. Many television sets include technology that allows you to block particular programs. Cable channels have added many new programs that compete with those on the regular networks. As a result, children's television now is much more diverse than it once was, and although cartoons and other animation still dominate, game shows, sports shows, animal shows, and news shows are also widely available. Even animal shows designed for adults may appeal to your young child. Now there are many more live shows for children, with both boys and girls as the main characters. Many shows depict boys and girls equally and show a broad representation of cultures and communities.

Television programs for young children appeal to the senses. Bright colors, speedy animation, fast action, fantasy, age-appropriate language, and engaging music all add to the attractiveness of the medium. But this means that television is sometimes mesmerizing. How often have you seen a young child sitting in front of the television set with what appears to be a glassy-eyed look? Clearly, television is a passive activity. Even though television for children has been greatly improved, it remains a one-sided communication that provides no opportunity for children to ask questions or formulate responses. There are things you can do to make watching television less passive and more of a language-learning experience. To begin with, you should try to watch some of the programs with your child so that television is no longer strictly used as a babysitting device. Watching programs together makes television into an activity in which there can be communication. Just as you have a conversation about a story that you have read aloud, so, too, can you have conversations about television programs. Ask questions like these:

- What did you like most about that program?
- Which character did you like the best? The least?
- If you could be a character, which one would you pick? Why?
- Did you like the way the program ended? Why?
- Can you think of a different ending?

Even during those times when your child watches a program alone, he needs to know that some adult may want to talk about the program, either immediately after it is over or, if that is not possible, then at a special time set aside for talking about what things were done during the day. If you did not see the program, you can ask your child to describe it and tell what she did or did not like about it and why. In addition, watching television can be the springboard for drawing and writing so that your child might even sketch a picture of something from a television program, and that can be the start of a conversation. The most important thing is to be sensitive to what your child is watching and not let television watching be the dominant event in your child's day.

Computers

Yes, the computer can be a learning tool. However, most four- to five-year-olds do not need a computer or electronic tablet of their own. Clearly, computer-based activities that encourage preschoolers to sit on an adult's lap and do something together are preferable to those that resemble television. While it is true that there is a wealth of software material available for the preschool age group, you need to be selective in what you purchase. Many apps and programs for children are based either on books or on familiar television programs. However, it is important to be aware that the commercialism of websites is not so different from the commercial pressure on television. Many of these sites contain a great deal of advertising.

Although using the computer can be more active than watching television, many of the same cautions that were noted above for television viewing still apply. A conversation about what is on the screen is a critical part of the experience. Although young children, particularly those who have older siblings, may want to experiment with the computer, parental involvement is essential. More detail on computer use for young children may be found in chapter 4, Young Readers and Writers.

In summary, not all activities that we described in this chapter are right for all preschool children. It is crucial to remember that while there are many possibilities, it is up to you to select those activities that are most appropriate for both you and your child. Follow her lead, and recognize the reality of your own busy life in figuring out the best way to enjoy some of these activities together.

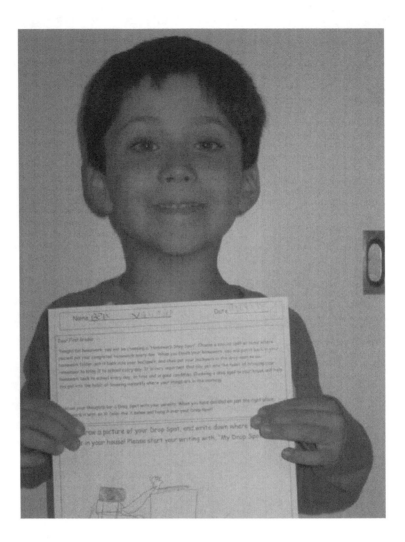

CHAPTER 4

YOUNG READERS AND WRITERS

Two mothers are having a brief conversation during the first two weeks of school. They are standing outside the school building, waiting to meet their kindergarten children.

Maryann: It seems so strange now that Mike is in school all day. I got used to doing things with him after he came home from morning preschool, and now I'm not sure if he's too tired or what.

Sally: I had the same feeling right after Kieran started all-day kindergarten. But then I just asked him what he would like to do. He had a lot of ideas.

Maryann: What did he want to do?

Sally: Well, his teacher had suggested some ideas. He wanted to go to the library, so now we go once a week. He loves to pick out books himself, and it gives me a chance to get some books for myself too.

Maryann: That sounds great. I'll ask Mike if he would like to go. Maybe we'll meet you, and the boys can pick out books together. Anything else you do together?

Sally: Well, Kieran likes to build things, so we went to a craft store, and he picked out a simple airplane model. We're going to work on it together. As we put it together, we can talk about the parts. Later, perhaps, we can even plan a trip on an airplane or just a visit to the local airport.

Maryann: Building models isn't something Mike likes to do, but now that I think about it, he does like to draw and paint. I guess it's time we went shopping for some new art supplies.

This conversation makes clear the changing role of parents as their children grow and begin formal schooling. At this stage, children have many ideas of their own, and it's important for us to follow their lead. Observe and ask your child what activities he is interested in, and involve him as an active participant in the planning. Conversation is a part of this planning process, and it's precisely here that reading and writing skills can be expanded. For example, Kieran and Mike may have had to look up the days and hours that the library is open and the best way for them to get there. Maryann and Mike will need to do a lot of planning before buying new art supplies. They'll probably first check to see what supplies they still have and then make a list of what to buy. They may need to look up the name of an art supply store and find out directions for getting there. If this involves a bus ride, there'll be many opportunities for using language.

In this chapter, we focus on the child's first years of formal schooling, beginning with kindergarten. It is in these first formal school years that learning to read and write are the critical activities. Although a few children may start school with some knowledge of reading and writing, these early school years provide the foundation for later learning. It is very important to understand that when children enter kindergarten, they do so at different ages, and therefore, their developmental stages are often different. For example, one child in kindergarten may be four years and eleven months old, while another in the same class may be five years and ten months old. In other words, the older child has lived for 20 percent more time than the younger child, meaning that their experiences and backgrounds are almost certain to vary greatly. Please keep these maturational differences in mind, and refrain from making any comparisons between your child and another.

Early school experiences, such as listening to stories and beginning to read simple stories, are crucial in developing the sense that "reading" is a fun thing to do. Without this understanding, it becomes difficult for children to become lifelong independent readers, writers, and thinkers.

Think about these questions as you read this chapter:

- What is my role as a parent during these early school years?
- What is special about five- and six-year olds?
- How do I communicate effectively with my child's teacher?
- How is reading and writing taught at this level?
- What can I do to further my child's interest in reading and writing?
- How can I use media as aids to learning?

Readers and Writers

Children of this age exhibit curiosity about the world around them. They begin to question the family routines they had previously accepted without demur. Questions such as, "Why do I have to go to bed now?" "Why can't you buy me that game?" and "Why is it night?" become increasingly frequent as the young school-age child becomes an independent thinker. It is at this age that children begin to think of themselves as male or female, think about right and wrong, and are increasingly involved in group play, with all of its rules.

Playing cooperatively and learning the rules require many experiences, and it is at this stage that friendships are formed. Group play at this age involves running, chasing, dodging, and jumping and allows children to feel a sense of mastery. It is also a time for learning how to take turns and share with friends, as well as with siblings. Also during this time most children tend to admire and emulate their parents and to take on some of the characteristics of one or both parents.

At this age, children are very social. They like to talk, invent games, organize and collect things, and recite silly songs and rhymes. They are usually filled with energy, very enthusiastic, generally happy, and eager to repeat jokes, a task that is often delightful. Every night at dinner, Greg, then a five-year-old, would ask, "Why did the chicken cross the road?" as if each night there would be a new response, but there wasn't. He would laugh, and his big sister, Buffy, would continually say, "We've heard that already." To which Greg would quickly try to make up a new ending. His family would laugh at his attempts, knowing that the next night the same thing would happen. This repeated conversation represented to Greg a sense of security and continuity, while above all, it made him the center of attention, something that a five-year-old can never manage to resist.

Young learners expand their understanding of longer stories that may involve more characters and more exciting plots. They also increase the details in their drawings of people, objects, and animals by adding unusual shapes and using more colors. Children of this age like to try new things and make their own decisions.

The six-year-old enters a stage of transition during which she is active, outgoing, and often very self-centered. Friends become increasingly important to her, and she'll have a preference for same-sex playmates. She likes rituals, rules, and playing with or taking care of younger children. The six-year-old likes to read and retell familiar stories. Although she likes to go to school, many children at this age often dawdle. As she enters this stage, she will begin the process of separating. Although highly social, five- and six-year-olds will sometimes simply need to get away and be by themselves. This process often starts with her mother, to whom she will direct her temper tantrums and whose directives she will often refuse. However, her empathy and attachment toward her mother are still very strong. During this transitional stage, the ability of the parent to maintain perspective and a sense of humor is vital.

The six-year-old's listening and speaking vocabulary doubles, and she is beginning to develop a longer attention span. Her ability to problem-solve emerges, and this needs to be strongly encouraged. Six-year-olds are generally just starting formal schooling, and parents are often concerned about the way their children reverse letters, such as *b* and *d*. The fact that they write stories with incorrect spelling, something that is frequently referred to as "invented" spelling, is a perfectly normal occurrence. At this stage, the ideas being expressed are more important than correct spelling and grammar, and you should not be overly concerned about it. They will begin to use conventional spelling as they acquire more and more experience with both reading and writing.

The Role of Parents

Clearly your parental role changes as your child grows, but observing and understanding your child remain essential components of it. As can be seen in the conversation between Sally and Maryann, your child needs to become an important part of any planning that you do for after-school and vacation time. While you may have many ideas for how to spend time with your child, sharing these ideas with him and listening to his ideas are critical. Sometimes your ideas will coincide; other times they will not. The important part here is the conversation the two of you have and the sharing of your ideas. This will become a model for when your child is older and needs to share his ideas with peers, siblings, and other adults in his environment. At this age, your child begins to test the limits of the adults around him. He needs you to explain things and show him how things work. Help your child to think about consequences, problems, and solutions in everyday events. Conversations about how he feels when things are going well or when he is having a problem are essential. These conversations help children understand their own behavior and feelings, what is expected of them, and how it affects others.

An additional but critical role relates to the school. Research has verified that children do better in school when their parents take an interest in and play an active role in their child's school. It is important to show that you are interested in what happens in your child's class and to talk to her when she comes home from school. Ask about the experiences and activities that went on in school that day. Look through your child's bag or backpack, and discuss some of the things that she brings home. If it is at all possible, you or a caregiver can volunteer to help out in your child's class. By fostering the home-school connection, you will provide a key component in the academic success of your child. We do, however, clearly recognize that many children will not be forthcoming with full responses to questions about their school day.

The following shows how one mother encouraged her child to share details about her day:

Mother:	Elaine, what did you do at school today?
Elaine:	Nothing much.
Mother:	When I was at work today, something really funny happened. [Mother relates funny incident], and it made the whole day more fun. Can you tell me something that made your day fun?
Elaine:	Oh yeah, we went out to the yard, and there was a bird who was flying around and making funny sounds.

How do you communicate information to your children's teachers? Early on in the school year, most schools have a back-to-school night. This is a time for parents and teachers to get to know each other and for the teachers to present an overview of the curriculum that they will be using throughout the school year. Since learning to read and write is a critical component of the curriculum at this level, you may have some questions about how the teacher plans to teach reading and writing. For example: Do the children work in small groups? Is there time for children to pick out books they want to read independently?

At this first meeting, you may be informed about upcoming special events, trips, or projects. The more you know about these events, the better you will be able to communicate with your child about them. If you take an interest, so, too, will your child. Ask about trips that are planned for the school year. Teachers always welcome parent involvement on out-of-school activities. Be sure, though, that if you go, you do not take on the role of "parent" on the trip; rather, your position will be that of an assistant to the teacher. And, of course and most important of all, do not focus on your child. Finally, your child's teacher may well distribute periodic updates or newsletters detailing the "goings on" of the class. If not, you might volunteer to help by taking on that role.

In addition to back-to-school night, most schools have one-on-one parent-teacher conferences during the school year, and these offer wonderful opportunities for you to communicate and establish a strong relationship with your child's teacher. This relationship will facilitate future communication, which is so important to your child's success in school. This is a time to raise any questions you have about the class curriculum, to indicate how your child reacts to school, to discuss the homework policy, and to become familiar with the teacher's expectations for your child. If you are a parent who works outside the home and has little time to participate in your child's class during the daytime, you can still be involved by attending parent-teacher conferences; volunteering for tasks that can be done at home, like collecting materials for a school project; and sharing information with other parents. Once you have begun to establish the lines of communication with your child's teacher, it will be easier to communicate when specific needs arise.

You obviously know your own child better than anyone else, and this knowledge can be of enormous benefit to your child's teacher, for whom it is important to be aware of any issues that may have an impact on a child's performance, attention, and motivation in school. For example, if a grandparent is very ill and the child is upset and distracted, the teacher needs to know about it so that school performance is judged accordingly. The teacher, too, may be able to help allay some of the child's concerns. If your child is struggling with homework, it is important for you not to do the work for him but rather to speak with his teacher, who perhaps can give your child more guidance in class.

Also, if your child continually comes home upset by something that has happened in school, you should inform his teacher. Notes sent to school generally are well received by teachers; phone calls are often less satisfactory and difficult for teachers to respond to, since they usually do not have ready access to a telephone during the day. Always give the teacher information about how best to reach you and ask her about the best way to contact her. Some teachers are open to receiving phone calls, emails, or text messages in the evening. If your child's teacher uses a computer, then email or a text message may prove the best way to communicate something critical that happened during the school day. Above all, it is important, even at this very early stage in your child's schooling, to forge a close parent-teacher partnership.

Another way to keep in touch with school policy and events is to set up a parent group. This can be an actual group of parents from your child's class that meets on a regular basis, or it can be an email network through which you can communicate with other parents. It is a way to stay knowledgeable about what is happening in school, as well as to share concerns with other parents. Frequently, another parent may have a solution to a problem that you are having with your child. This group contact becomes particularly important if your child is ill and misses classroom instruction, as other parents, as well as the teacher, can keep you up to date on classwork and assignments.

A Focus on Reading and Writing

It is critical that you as a concerned parent are knowledgeable about the reading and writing curriculum that is being used in the classroom. You may live in a community in which there is a district-wide policy regarding reading and writing, in which case the type of books used, the amount of time devoted to literacy each day, and the specific teaching methods are all mandated. On the other hand, your community may be more decentralized, with decisions about reading and writing made at the school level. And in some schools, individual teachers have the authority to develop and implement their own reading and writing programs. What is important to you as a parent is to be knowledgeable about some of the terms used in the teaching of reading and writing so that you will be comfortable in discussing programs with other parents, the classroom teacher, or the building administrator.

Learning to Read

Learning to read is the major focus of the early grades. Early on, children develop many language and cognitive skills that form the foundation for learning to read and write. At this stage, children are called "young readers," and as such, your child may be learning to read using a basal reader series. This is a set of books from a commercial publisher in which the vocabulary and stories are designed for a specific grade. In the early grades, the stories are very simple, with easy vocabulary and many pictures. Each book is accompanied by a teacher's manual or guidebook and a workbook containing a variety of activities for the children. The children, generally in small groups of about five or six, read the story with the teacher, discuss it, and answer questions. They may do follow-up writing or drawing activities as suggested in the teacher's manual, or the teacher may develop activities of her own. In some classrooms that use a basal reading series, teachers also use "big books." These are oversized storybooks that enable a group of students to work together with the teacher on a story. In some cases, "little books" of the same story are available so that the children can reread the story independently or with a partner.

In many classrooms today, phonics programs are used as supplementary materials or, in rare cases, as the major learning-to-read program. These materials are designed to aid children in acquiring the sound-symbol relationships of the printed letters. These programs tend to be free of context so that children focus only on letters and words. In our opinion, learning to read using only a phonics program is too limiting and needs to be supplemented with good stories that focus on the meaning of the text and that interest the children enough to inspire them to want to read. Furthermore, for those children who enter school already knowing how to read, phonics instruction is irrelevant and may actively discourage them from reading for fun. For example, we liken this to what happens if you buy a new DVD player. If you already know how to use it, you might not need to read the instruction manual. If, however, you do not know how to use it, you would need to read the manual. Likewise, the use of phonics instruction should be confined to only those who need it. It is also important to realize that phonics instruction is a very auditory process, one which requires the learner to hear discrete differences in sounds, and the fact is that at this age, not all children's auditory acuity is at the same development level. The result is that for some children, a purely phonetic approach to instruction may not be advisable at all.

We advocate a balanced reading program beginning in the early grades and continuing throughout the elementary school years. This would include phonics instruction only for those children who need it—that is, as a tool for learning to read but not as the reading program itself. As children progress from being young readers to mature readers, understanding stories and the important ideas in science and social studies materials is the goal of a balanced reading program. Constructing meaning from what is being read, learning to be a critical reader, and knowing that reading can be fun are how children develop into lifelong readers.

Reading Aloud
It has been well documented that reading aloud to children fosters their reading, writing, listening, and speaking abilities. Reading

aloud is generally part of the curriculum in the early grades. Indeed, both a school and a home focus on reading aloud are critical to the emerging reader. We hope that you have been reading to your child before he entered school, but whether you did so or not, it is vitally important to read to him now, since when you read a book aloud to him, it exposes him to a wide variety of experiences. Your child will probably have a few books that he wants to hear over and over again, and after multiple readings, he will most likely be able to re-peat much of the story. This is a very important step that should be encouraged, even if your child does not recreate the story with com-plete accuracy. Perhaps the most important things that you can do at this stage are to observe your child, celebrate his attempts at lit-eracy, provide lots of encouragement, and serve as a model.

When you and your child sit together, begin by looking at the cover and the pictures. Always make sure that you are sitting close enough so that your child can easily see the pages. Ask him what he thinks the book will be about. This will help him develop an ability to predict and interpret the things that he reads. As you read, be sure to discuss the ideas in the book, remembering to take your time and enable your child to look at the pictures. Allow him to ask you ques-tions and to interrupt as you read. In order to keep this from being a passive activity, ask him to help by turning the pages, pointing to things, or repeating some of the text. Most important, however, is for you to observe your child. If he seems uninterested, then you should stop reading. Remember, this is supposed to be a pleasurable ex-perience for both of you! It is perfectly all right to close a book and discuss what your child did not like about it. These critical reading skills will serve him well as he progresses in literacy.

One parent we know, a teacher herself, often read to her child. However, when her child began to pick up books and "make believe" she was reading, she noticed that her daughter began at the back of the book and turned pages from right to left. It was only then that her mother realized that even though she had continually read to her, she really hadn't "modeled" reading behaviors with her. Here are some things you can do to model:

- Look at the cover of the book and the title on the front page.
- Turn the pages together.
- Point to the words and phrases as you read from left to right.
- Point out repeated or key words in the story.
- Look at the pictures and discuss them.

Children understand stories at a much higher level than those stories they can read by themselves. As you read, you will help stimulate your child's listening ability, increase his comprehension and vocabulary, and at the same time heighten his interest in and awareness of books. Perhaps most importantly, you will be conveying your own appreciation for and interest in reading. The books you choose should be those that are of interest to both you and your child, so visit a library or local bookstore and select books together. Some children of this age enjoy picture books and books with rhymes, patterns, or repeated text, while others of the same age are ready to listen to simple chapter books. Your child may begin to recognize some words or letters at this stage. If time permits, it is beneficial for you to read the book to yourself first, since by doing so you will become familiar with the content and also be better prepared to read it with expression and understanding. Using various intonations where appropriate will also enhance the reading experience for your child and help maintain his interest.

A critical part of reading aloud to your child is the conversation that takes place before reading, during reading, and after the story is completed. This conversation is what makes reading aloud both an enjoyable experience and a learning experience. Matt and his son Philippe have spent the last few days reading a chapter book entitled *Good Morning, Gorillas* by Mary Pope Osborne.

About a week before they started to read this book, the family visited the zoo, and Philippe became fascinated with the gorillas. He wanted to know how they talked to each other and where they slept. As a result, his dad picked up two paperbacks about go-rillas the next time he was in a bookstore. One, *Gorillas* by Patricia Demuth, is a nonfiction book. The second book, *Good Morning, Gorillas*, is a storybook. Matt noted that it is number twenty-six in a series of books in which eight-year-old Jack and his seven-year-old sister, Annie, have a magic tree house filled with books, which takes them to the places described in the books. Matt thought that if Philippe liked this book, they could read others in the same series. Matt decided to save the nonfiction book about gorillas to read after they have finished the fiction book. It is interesting to note that Matt chose a chapter book. Although Philippe is still a young reader, it won't be long before he'll be able to read simple chapter books on his own.

This evening they are reading chapter 5, entitled "Silverback." Before they started this chapter, Matt asked Philippe if he remembered what happened in chapter 4. Philippe responded that Jack had left his sister with a baby gorilla and he couldn't find her.

"That's right," said Matt. "Let's see if he finds Annie in this chapter."

Matt has read the beginning of chapter 5. The excerpt below is from the middle of the chapter to the end.

Matt:	Look's like Bubu, the baby gorilla, is helping Jack find Annie. Wow! Jack looks scared in that picture.
Philippe:	Yeah! Really scared. I would be too.
Matt:	Let's see what happens next.

The silverback growled again. His long, shaggy arms touched the ground. His fingers curled under. Walking on his knuckles, he stepped toward Jack.
Jack stepped back.

Matt: Sounds scary. What do you think will happen now?

Philippe: I think the gorilla will help Jack to find Annie.

Matt: (reading): The gorilla stepped forward. Jack kept stepping back until he had stepped out of the clearing. But, the silverback kept coming. Jack stumbled through brush until he came to a thick wall of plants.

Matt: What would you do if you were Jack?

Philippe: I would hide, or maybe run very fast.

Matt: How would you feel?

Philippe: Really scared.

Matt: OK. Let's see what Jack does.

Matt (reading): The gorilla kept coming. Jack couldn't move
back anymore. "Uh, uh," he said nervously. He
held up his hand. "I come in—"
Before Jack could say "peace" the giant gorilla went crazy.
He hooted and leaped to his feet.
Jack crouched down in panic. The gorilla kept hooting. He
grabbed a tree limb. He shook it wildly. He ripped
leaves from the branches. He gnashed his teeth.
He cupped his hands. He beat his chest.
Wraagh! he roared. Wraagh!
Matt: Can you roar like a gorilla?
Philippe (beating his chest): Wraagh! Wraagh!
Matt (reading): The gorilla dropped on all fours. He charged
back and forth past Jack. Then he threw himself
on his belly. He began bashing the ground with
his palms. He bashed and bashed and bashed.
Matt: Wow! He sounds angry to me. Do you know what
the word *bashed* means?
Philippe: Like banging—sometimes I bang my head when I
get mad.
Matt: That's right.
Matt (reading): Jack scrambled on his hands and knees over
to a tree. He hid behind the trunk, hugging his
head. He waited for the maniac gorilla to find him
and tear him to pieces.
Matt: Well, that's the end of chapter 5. I see Jack didn't
find Annie yet. What do you think will happen to
Jack and Annie in chapter 6?
Philippe: I don't know. Can we read another chapter now?
Matt: No, it's kinda late. Let's save it for tomorrow.

This excerpt of a conversation between Matt and his son Philippe demonstrates several techniques you can use with children of this age to add learning experiences to the pleasure of reading aloud.

These techniques, which are useful regardless of what you have chosen to read, include the following:

- Choose a story that relates to the child's own experience or interests, as Matt did.
- Ask a question, and have a brief conversation before beginning to read. If you are reading a chapter book, talk about the previous chapter.
- Stop reading to answer your child's questions.
- Stop reading and ask about the meaning of a word that you think is difficult.
- Stop reading at critical points, either to clarify or to elaborate on something in the story.
- Stop reading to talk about a character and how that character makes you and your child feel.
- Stop reading to ask a question about the story and predict what may happen next. Then read on to see if the prediction was accurate.
- Stop near the end of a chapter, and ask your child what he thinks will happen in the next chapter.

When you finish reading the book, the conversation may focus on one or more aspects of the story. Any of the following questions can spark an engaging conversation with your child, but don't forget that the conversation is one in which you participate as well. Be ready with your own answers and with your comments and reflections on your child's point of view.

- Did you like the book? Why?
- Was there a character you especially liked? What about a character you thought was mean, or scary, or that you just didn't like at all?
- Was there a part of the book that you especially liked or disliked? (You may choose to reread the part that was especially liked.)
- Did the book end the way you thought it would?

- Did you like the ending? Why?
- If you wrote this book, would you give it a different ending?
- Would you like to read other books with the same characters? (This question assumes you are reading a book from a series.)

Just Talking Together

Sometimes just an unplanned conversation between you and your child leads to new understanding. Here are two conversations, only one of which expands the child's knowledge. A father and his six-year-old son, James, begin to talk as their plane comes in for landing on one of the Hawaiian Islands.

Father: Look down at the water. Can you see all the colors?

James: There's lots of blue water, but the colors are different. Why is that?

Father: Well, it depends on how deep the water is. Where the water is very deep, the color is much darker.

James: Will I be able to see the colors when we go swimming?

Father: I'm not sure. Let's remember to look tomorrow.

Although this conversation was initiated by an adult, it apparently held strong interest for a young child and may well have led to further exploration of water and its properties.

By way of contrast, here is an example of a missed language opportunity. A father and his six-year-old daughter, Susan, were approaching the animal-petting area at a local zoo.

Father: Do you wanna pet?

Susan: I want a pet! I want a pet! I don't want to pet anything.

The father made no response but just kept on walking to the petting area. It is clear from the way Susan responded to her father that she was well aware of the difference in the use of the words "wanna pet." She interpreted the word "wanna" as "want a" not "want to." She used appropriate stress as she differentiated between wanting a pet of her own and going to pet the animals. This was an excellent time for her father to have conversed with his daughter in a way that showed that he fully understood her distinction in meaning and to praise her for her use of the English language. Maybe even a good time to inquire as to what kind of pet she wanted. Perhaps he already knew what kind of pet she wanted and was deliberately ignoring her.

Encouraging Writing

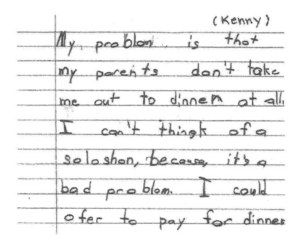

(Kenny)
My problen is that my parents don't take me out to dinnem at all. I can't thingk of a soloshon, becouse it's a bad problom. I could ofer to pay for dinner

The young reader begins to write about things that interest him. He may share his writing with other students, keep it in a journal, or take it home to show you. Writing at this stage generally contains invented spelling and drawings. The following writing samples are from two six-year-old boys near the end of grade one. They have just listened to a story about a boy who had a problem. The teacher encouraged the children to talk about the story and then to write about a problem that they themselves had had.

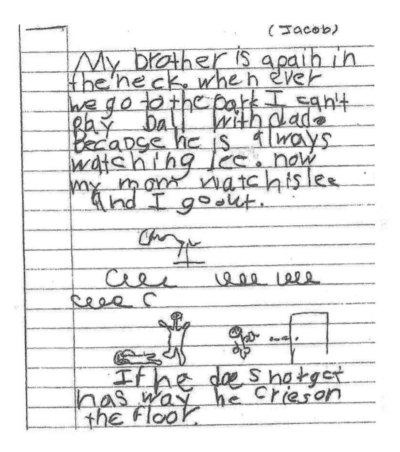

(Jacob)

My brother is apain in the neck. when ever we go to the park I can't phy ball with dad. becaude he is always watching lee. now my mom watch islee and I go out.

If he does not get has way he cries on the floor.

It is interesting to note that even though these two boys are in the same grade, their writing shows many differences. Kenny uses the vocabulary that was discussed in class (problem and solution), but it is clear that Jacob understands the concept as well. Both boys use invented spelling (*problim, soloshon, ofer, becauz*), but we have no difficulty in understanding their communications. Both of them use contractions correctly in the word *can't*. Kenny seems to have more knowledge of punctuation and uses periods and capital letters correctly, whereas this aspect is somewhat less developed in Jacob's writing. Jacob has added some drawings to illustrate his story, while Kenny did not feel so inclined.

Further, Kenny and Jacob not only understood what a problem is and how one might solve it, but they were able to relate the ideas in the story to a problem of their own. They clearly expressed their ideas, even though they did not use all the conventional spelling and punctuation of the English language. When Jacob and Kenny bring their stories home, they need to be praised for their ideas, encouraged to write more, and accepted for their use of invented spelling and less-than-perfect punctuation. Remember that your child's ability to use correct spelling and punctuation will increase as he reads more and has increasing opportunities for writing both in school and at home. You might even share a problem that you have had and how you solved it as a follow-up to the concept that the teacher has been developing.

Here are some more examples of encouraging writing at home. Siri's mother encourages her daughter to draw and write by having paper, crayons, and markers available both at home and when they travel. After Siri and her family returned from a trip to Florida, she drew this picture:

When asked to tell about her drawing, Siri said, "I liked all the flowers we saw. There were coconuts falling down from the tree. We stayed in a big hotel."

Here is a sample of a get-well card that Siri sent to her grandfather when he was ill at home:

Dear GrandPaharvex
Get Better
Miss you Very SooN, I
Love you Much.

Siri, age six, enjoys drawing and writing and is eager to talk about what she has done. She has a very attentive audience, since both her parents and grandparents strongly encourage her work and are proud to place it on a bulletin board or on the refrigerator door for others to see. As a parent whose goal it is to encourage your child to read and write, the most important things for you to remember are to praise your child's work, accept the use of invented spelling and incorrect grammar, and provide as many opportunities as you possibly can for writing.

Things to Do at Home

Classrooms are not the only places where children learn to read and write. Your home is a key environment in which children's literacy development can be encouraged and enhanced. You should always have paper and pencils or crayons available, and it would be advantageous if these were stored in an area that is easily accessible by your child. You should also have a special place in which your child's books are stored. While a bookcase may be preferable, even a storage box is good. Here, too, it is important that your child be able to get to it himself.

Magnetic letters spark word and story play, as can a chalkboard if you have one. Your child may ask you to spell out a word, or you may discuss words or pictures placed on the refrigerator where he can see them. It may be something that you are cooking that he will want you to spell out. You might highlight a letter of the day, and as both of you go through your various regular activities, think about what words or things begin with that letter. You can find pictures in a magazine or a recipe that begin with the letter of the day. You can take a fresh small paper bag, label it with the letter of the day, and then help your child cut out pictures of things that start with that letter and place them in the bag.

As your child begins to develop as a reader, you can create a personalized picture dictionary. Help him write a letter of the alphabet on the top of each page in a notebook or loose-leaf-type book. You and he can then put pictures and the corresponding words on the page. Family photographs can also be put in this dictionary. This is especially helpful as your child begins to write thank-you notes or send emails to friends and relatives.

Grocery shopping is a wonderful opportunity for you and your child. Writing your grocery list can be a shared activity, with him writing his own list or dictating items to add to your list. After school, the two of you can reread the list and check off the items you bought while he was in school, with particular emphasis on the items that your child wanted. This may lead to a conversation about why you were unable to purchase certain items, why you substituted one item for another, and which items on the list need to be repeated for the next shopping expedition.

Here are some other things you can do at home to help encourage reading and writing as a way of communicating:

- Write notes to and with your child. If you pack a lunch for your child, your note might just include a word or two with a simple picture. It also helps your child connect with you during the school day.

- When your child receives a gift, you and he could write or email a thank-you note together. If he is not yet able to write or use the computer, then let him dictate it to you.

- Keep a memo board handy. You can use a magnetic chalkboard and place it on your refrigerator. As your child watches, mark down special dates and events. When he is ready, encourage him to note things on the board.

- Make homemade greeting cards, such as a birthday card for a friend or relative. This is a simple way to connect speaking and writing.

- Create invitations to your child's birthday party together. Cut out pictures from magazines, such as animals, flowers, or food, and paste them on blank paper that has been folded in four parts, writing the party facts inside.

- Initiate a family journal, where all members of the family draw or insert a photo, along with a few words or sentences.

- If you have an animal at home (e.g., a cat, a dog, a hamster, or tropical fish), encourage your child to draw, write, or dictate something he knows about the animal. Write down what he dictates so he can read it back to you. Also, your child may understand the concept of "responsibility" if he has some specific chore to do for the animal, like helping to feed the fish or checking to see if the dog has enough water. Perhaps when the two of you are at the library, you can look for a book about the animal.

Here is an example of a letter written by a mother to her daughter Esther and Esther's response:

> Dear Esther,
>
> Did you have fun on your sleepover at Grandma's? Daddy and I went to see a movie downstairs in North Shore Towers and then we went home. The movie was about German Jews who ran away from the Nazi's and went to Kenya, in Africa.
>
> This batch of worms was really good, wasn't it? Is camp getting to be more fun as you make some new friends? Michelle is supposed to come to work this week. Hopefully, I'll get a lot of writing done this week. I really want to send out at least one article this week—
>
> I love you,
> Mommy

Dear Mom,
I had a ball, at
Grandma's house.
I hope you liked the
movie.
That was a very yes
good batch of worms.
Thank you for
the make up, I realy
like it. Some times I put it
on my barbiess.

Sarah has this red
head book I read half
of it it is called the
Chocolate Touch
love,
Esther

It is very possible that, given Esther's language abilities, it will be necessary for an adult to read her mother's letter to her. Esther should be able to read her response as she wrote it. Letter writing is an excellent way of expanding a child's vocabulary and concepts. As the letters are read, a conversation about the ideas is essential.

Cooking together is a fun activity, so encourage your child to cook a dish with you. There are many cookbooks for children, and this is a wonderful way to encourage not only reading but also math. Be sure, though, that when you do decide to cook together, you have allowed plenty of time and are feeling patient. Your child will undoubtedly make a mess, but the experience will be worth it. One idea is to devise a menu together, listing the parts of the meal you will be serving. Be sure to include some of your child's favorite dishes. If you do this way ahead of time, you can list the ingredients you will need, and you can then go to the supermarket to buy them together.

Ask your child for help in getting the ingredients out of the pantry or refrigerator. Read the labels together, and point out key words. Talk about the amount of each ingredient that the recipe calls for, and measure them together. Another idea is to cook a theme dinner or a special dish related to a book that you have read. For example, after reading *Charlie and the Chocolate Factory* by Roald Dahl, you might plan to bake a chocolate cake or make chocolate pudding.

Some Additional Ideas

Even though your child is in school full time now, there's still time for playing games, and there are many literacy-related ones that you can play, both in the home and outside, costing little or no money.

- Play "Seek and Spell." You point out something that you see, then ask him to guess the letter it starts with (or spell it if he is able). You can play this while driving in the car or just taking a walk.
- Play "I'm thinking of..." Think of an object or something that you have seen on a previous trip or neighborhood walk and have him guess what it is. You might begin with some clue such as, "I'm thinking of a store that sells food." Reverse the process, and let him think of something he saw.
- Play "Pick a Letter." (Hint: start with consonants.) Try to identify as many things as you can starting with that letter.

If you work outside the home, we encourage you to take your child to your place of employment if that is at all possible. Point out what you do and how and why you do certain things, showing her that reading and writing are integral parts of your workday. Not only will experiences such as this help her with her own reading and writing, but they will also better enable her to understand what you do, to feel part of your workday, and to share in your experiences. If you cannot take your child to your workplace, then perhaps you can share photos of your workplace with her. You can even turn these pictures into a book with simple sentences that you can read together.

Going on Trips

Almost all children of this age enjoy trips, whether long or short. Traveling away from home creates prime opportunities for enriching your child's reading, writing, listening, and speaking abilities. Distractions such as television and phone calls are eliminated on most trips, giving you more opportunity to talk together and expand your child's vocabulary and concepts as you explore new places together. In chapter 5, Evolving Readers and Writers, we detail many language experiences, beginning with planning a trip and concluding with follow-up activities. Please refer to this chapter and select those activities that are most appropriate for your child from the section entitled "Going on Trips" pp. 119-122..

Using Media

Television and Movies

During the past decade, we have seen much improvement in the quality and appeal of television shows. Many network and cable stations have excellent programs that enhance children's learning. However, television watching is still a one-sided, passive activity. Nevertheless, television viewing can be used as an important adjunct to your child's educational development.

For a start, watch some programs with your child. During the commercials, you might discuss what is being advertised and how to evaluate a product. If you are watching a program with a story line, you might want to use the commercial time to predict what might happen next. Using television viewing as an experience that parallels reading a book gives you an opportunity for a conversation about the content.

Here are some questions you might use to stimulate your conversation:

- Did you like the program? Why?
- What did you like or dislike about it?
- Is this anything you have ever done?
- Which character did you like the best? The least? Why?
- If you could be one of the characters, which one would you choose? Why?
- What did you think about the ending? Did you like it? Why or why not?
- If you were writing the show, how might you have changed the ending?

Additional details on television viewing may be found in chapter 3, Your Preschool Child on pp. 63-64.

Going to the movies with your child is very similar to watching television together. Select the movie that you both will see by getting a recommendation from friends or by reading reviews in the local newspaper that you have shared with your child. After you have both watched the movie, you can use the same sample questions noted above as you walk or drive home. Remember, there are no correct answers.

With adult supervision and guidance, we feel confident that both television watching and moviegoing can be activities that increase children's understanding of the world they live in.

Using the Computer

Computers, like other media, can have both a positive and negative impact on your child's learning and socialization. In our highly technological society, many parents worry that if their children are not computer literate at an early age, they will find themselves at a disadvantage. This is not so. The decision as to whether or not to buy a computer should be based on your personal and financial situation. Do not purchase one just for your kindergartner. If you have one, fine. If you don't, that's fine too.

If you have a computer and you would feel comfortable allowing your child to use it, remember that he will not be as fastidious as you. Make sure that you are not concerned with fingerprints, the possibility of a bit of mess on the keyboard, or something as simple as software programs taking up more hard drive space. If you are replacing a computer, you might want to keep your old one and have that dedicated for use by your child.

As you preview and select computer programs for your preschool child, make sure that you include her in the evaluation and selection process whenever possible. There are many wonderful programs for children of this age, but make sure that the programs you select are of interest to your child, are on her developmental level, do not include violent content, and involve her in some hands-on activities. Avoid buying any programs that claim that your child will become smarter or read better as a result of using them. Select instead those programs that are interactive and engage your child in thinking. Programs that encourage creativity, imagination, and exploration and come with sound, music, and good graphics should be a priority.

Be sure that the programs you purchase are not too difficult for your child to use without assistance. It is also important to make sure that the program is not one that your child will use a few times and then outgrow, so look for programs that have varying activities at different levels of difficulty. Initially, programs for children of this age should be simple to operate, ones that they can navigate through on their own with just a point or click of the mouse.

As you do with books, make sure you're available to interact with your child as he works at the computer, to answer questions, and generally to talk about the program and its components. Try not to tell him what to do and how to do it. Rather, encourage him to figure out by himself what needs to be done. Be supportive rather than overbearing! Try to relate things done in and with the computer program to things that you and your child normally do. Talk about the letters, words, colors, and shapes in the program, using it as a springboard for further discussions and explorations. Computers are wonderful tools for reading and writing, and even at his age, he may be able to use one to begin writing a short story, an invitation, or a thank-you note.

One way to use the computer together with your son or daughter is for you to keep a computerized shopping list in a computer file. For example, Kathy, who loves to go to the supermarket with her mother, Cindy, reads the computerized shopping list before they leave and, together with her mother, modifies it according to their current needs. As Kathy becomes more familiar with the supermarket, they can categorize and sort the list so that it is easier to shop once they are in the store. Sorting, classifying, and categorizing are very important skills, and they are ones that can be easily facilitated with the computer by using clip art and the editing functions (cut, copy, and paste) on the computer.

Another activity that parents and children can do together occurs when the content of the program is a story. In this case, you can use many of the same activities that we have suggested for watching television, going to the movies, and read-alouds, described in detail in previous chapters in the sections on reading and writing.

One of the problems that we see is that computer use itself, for far too many children, becomes a solitary activity, sometimes interfering with socialization, which is so important at this age. If your child can work with another child at the computer, it will foster important social skills such as taking turns, patience, fairness, and cooperation. Programs that encourage multiple users, negotiation, language skills, problem-solving, and interaction by participants are most beneficial. But above all, if he is using the computer, he should find it an enjoyable, positive experience.

Using the Library

Time spent together at the library is a very special time, one that needs to be jointly celebrated by both you and your child. Carrie, a seven-year-old, fondly recalls her first visits to the library with her mother, Erica, who sat nearby as she looked through books. When planning a visit to the library, be sure to allow plenty of time for your child to walk around and look at the many books on the shelves. Encourage her to pick out some books and to sit down and preview them. You may decide to sit with her as she previews the books and talk with her about them or let her independently decide which ones she would like to borrow.

Through subsequent visits, you will probably begin to see patterns of preferences. Your child may select only picture books, or she may select books that she will want you to read aloud at home. Of course you may suggest a book to her, especially if it's one you remember fondly from your own childhood. You may also notice that she takes out the same book several times. This is fine. Remember that the goal is to develop and heighten her awareness and interest in books and related print materials.

The library today is a place where librarians have become aware of the need for children to be active and engaged in listening, speaking, and reading experiences. Modern libraries have a wealth of materials besides books. Newspapers, magazines, videos, DVDs, LEGO bricks, and even stuffed animals are an important part of many children's sections. Many of these are companions to books that you can borrow to further enhance your child's interaction with the characters and ideas she has viewed.

In addition to audiovisual materials, many libraries have special programs for children of all ages. When you speak with the children's librarian, you'll find out if your local library offers any, such as author visits, librarian reading favorite stories aloud, movies, LEGO contests, or arts and book workshops where children are engaged in book-related activities. If your local library does not offer any special events for children, ask them to consider it, and encourage other parents in your community to communicate their ideas to the local city board responsible for the public library.

This chapter has focused on the young reader and writer who is at a critical stage in the development of literacy. The knowledge and skills that are developed at this age form the foundation for later learning. As a parent, you have the role of being responsive to your child's needs and supportive of her school activities so that she may grow up to be open to new ideas, people, and places.

CHAPTER 5

Evolving Readers and Writers

Two mothers, Donna and Carolina, are sitting in the employee cafeteria having lunch and discussing their children.

Donna:	I don't know what's wrong with Joanna these days. She loved reading in second grade, but now that she's in third grade, she says that everything is just boring.
Carolina:	That same thing happened to Pablo, but now things seem to be OK.
Donna:	Did you do anything to help when he was bored?
Carolina:	Well, I did a lot of different things, and he loves to read on his own now and says the books in school are interesting. One of the things that we did was go to the library. I let him pick out any books he wanted. When we came home, if the book seemed too hard for him to read on his own, I read it aloud to him. Then we talked about the characters. He seemed to enjoy that a lot, especially if the main character was a boy who got into trouble at home.
Donna:	I guess Joanna and I could do that. Did you bother to speak to his teacher?
Carolina:	I thought about writing a note to his teacher, but then I just waited until we had a conference. I did

> mention to his teacher that he was bored in class, and she said that she would try to find some books that he would like. I guess she did that because things did seem to get better as the school year went on.
>
> Donna: I think I'll make an appointment now to see Joanna's teacher. I don't think I'll wait for the regular teacher conferences.

This conversation between these two mothers shows us the importance of parental involvement, especially during a child's early school years. Both mothers are aware of their children's school activities and take advantage of teacher meetings. Effectively communicating with your child's teacher is an excellent way to know what is happening in school and to get suggestions for activities to do at home that will further enhance your child's reading and writing. It is also important not to wait if you think that a problem is developing. A meeting early in the school year can help both you and your child's teacher to better understand your child. This meeting is useful in that you will learn about the reading program that is being used and the emphasis that the teacher plans to put on language activities.

In this chapter, we'll describe activities to expand children's interests in a variety of books and also consider ways to use television, movies, and the computer as aids to developing reading and writing abilities. It is in grades two and three that your child uses those reading and writing skills that she acquired in kindergarten and grade one. Now, as she becomes an evolving reader, reading on her own begins to take up more time, and she begins to appreciate that reading is fun. Since this is the stage of development that can lead children into becoming independent and lifelong readers and writers, we include many suggestions for family experiences that will motivate children to read widely and to write about their experiences.

Think about these questions as you read this chapter:
- Who is the developing reader and writer?
- How does my role as a parent change as my child gets older?
- What are some family activities that will enhance my child's literacy?
- How can I foster independent reading and writing?
- What is the place of the media in my child's life?

Readers and Writers

Before talking about reading and writing for children at this stage, it is important to understand their typical characteristics. Many children at these ages become introverted, and some have low levels of confidence in themselves. They are contemplative and thoughtful and often focus on themselves and their physical well-being and safety. A seven-year-old may respond to questions with simply, "I don't know," or "We haven't learned that yet." The seven-year-old will constantly ask, "Why?" This is a precursor to her development of more logical and abstract thinking that occurs during the subsequent year. The seven-year-old child is often very hard on herself—she wants to do things right, she wants to "be perfect," and she gets very upset when that doesn't happen. This impacts her performance and attitude in school. Children at this age will empathize with characters in a story or movie. They may often become emotionally attached to such characters. As your child matures, she will also want more independence, both socially and educationally.

At this age, children begin to separate home and school, and their learning styles begin to emerge. Some children prefer to work independently, while others like to participate in group projects. Most seven-and eight-year-olds like to participate in hands-on activities. Some work quickly, while others need time. This is not anything that they can control, but rather it is the emergence of their own style. Reading ability and spelling ability often vary greatly, with reading proficiency exceeding spelling. Third graders often exhibit proficiency in reading and enjoy reading on their own. They speak more eloquently than they write, and spelling and grammar may continue to be troublesome for them.

By third grade, children like a variety of educational experiences. In school, they enjoy working in learning centers. Children of this age usually enjoy school and the socialization with their peers. If their classroom involves them in learning activities rather than passive work sheet-type experiences, they may even prefer school to home. Third graders often exhibit proficiency in reading and enjoy reading on their own. The third grader will usually want to discuss her day and share her educational experiences with others. She takes great pride and delight when a parent or caregiver helps out in the classroom.

It is very important to remember these characteristics, since they can greatly impact your child's school performance and your interactions about it. For example, when your child writes a draft of a story, if you or your child's teacher place too much emphasis on correct spelling and grammar, it may hamper the thought process and curtail creativity. Please remember to distinguish between drafts and final products in writing. If too much emphasis is placed on correct spelling, then most children will use basic words that they know are right rather than using words from their more advanced oral language. One third grader we know was writing a story about dinosaurs, and when it was pointed out that he spelled *dinosaur* wrong, he changed the focus of the story to dogs. Let your child's expanded oral vocabulary flow, and when final versions are due, then spelling and grammar can be corrected. The most important part of writing is getting the thoughts on paper—the rest can follow.

The Role of Parents

Your role as a parent begins to change as your child matures. Your child needs independence but also needs to know that you are always there for support. Some children balk at parents helping them with homework; others want such help. Take your lead from your child. Perhaps one of the most important things to do as a parent is to be an active listener. By listening, we show our children that we value what they say and care about them and their thoughts. Share your values, viewpoints, dreams, and interests, and listen to hers. Dinnertime is a good time to talk about things, but not if there is the distraction of television. Let the distractions of the day fall away, and focus on you and your child. Encourage her to discuss her day at school, but don't pressure her to provide information all the time. Be sure to talk about what you have done in your day as well and any concerns that you may have about something at work. This will open up lines of communication. If you made an error at work, share that with her. This will show her that it is all right to make mistakes and to talk about them. One time during dinner, Carole said that she felt stupid because of something that happened at work. Buffy, her daughter, picked up on this and tried to comfort her by saying, "You're not stupid, Mom, you just did a stupid thing." This then sparked a conversation about mistakes and how they make us feel. By talking about your concerns, you are modeling the kind of behavior that you want your child to exhibit.

Parents often feel that they should fill afternoons or weekends with structured activities for their children. Working parents tend to feel this even more. It is important to realize that children need time to just relax or do things spontaneously. Running errands together and talking is just as beneficial as going to a museum. There is plenty of time as children grow to incorporate activities such as art classes, gymnastics, or swimming lessons into their day. We are not saying do not expose your children to activities; rather, we are encouraging you to carefully select and moderate your children's after-school activities and not overwhelm them.

Your child's interests and desires will emerge at this age, and it is important to recognize them and help design activities that are in sync with them. Museums geared specifically toward children are a wonderful way to introduce your child to the world of art, science, and so on. Zoos, too, are often favored by children of this age. Remember to take your lead from your child. If she is not interested in something at this stage, wait a year or two and try it again. Whether you visit a venue specifically for children or one that is generic, the most important thing you can do is talk to your child. Ask her what she likes, what she doesn't like, and why. Discuss your feelings about what you're seeing, and make sure that she feels comfortable disagreeing with you.

Let's look at the following conversation that took place when Barry took his young son, Greg, to a special concert designed for youngsters:

Greg:	I really liked that music. What was its name?
Barry:	It's called *The Four Seasons*.
Greg:	That's a funny name for music. Aren't the seasons part of the weather?
Barry:	Yes, they are, but the composer wanted to give you the "feel" of the seasons. How do you feel in winter and in summer?
Greg:	In winter, I feel cold, but in summer, I feel hot. Now I get it! That's why the music was different each time.
Barry:	When we get home, let's listen to it again and see if we get a sense of each of the four seasons.
Greg:	That will be fun! We can make hot chocolate when we listen to the wintry part, and then we can have ice cream when we listen to the summery part.

Cultural events are not the only ways to facilitate and encourage learning at this age. Explorations can be as simple as taking a walk together in an unfamiliar neighborhood. Anita and her daughter, Mary, age eight, had the following experience when they passed a new house. Mary started talking about the flowers in the garden and said that she wished they could have flowers like that. They talked about the colors, the fragrances, and the care of plants, and subsequently they decided to buy some plants and try their hand at horticulture. Anita recalls that she never realized that Mary had any interest in flowers and that it was this unique opportunity that brought this to her attention. Above all, it is important to allow your child the opportunity to explore things both with you and on her own.

Allow your child to try new experiences, and encourage her to take safe risks. We encourage you to take an active interest in and help your child with a school project, but too often educators see projects that were done mostly by parents. Please bear in mind that if you offer too much help to your child, it may convey to her a sense that she is incapable or that things always have to be perfect, and either of these impressions will erode her self-confidence. She will also get little satisfaction from a good grade if you have done the work for her. Rather, work with her, but let her do the majority of the work.

For example, many years ago Bobby had to do a book-related project. Rather than him writing a book report with his mother's intervention, his teacher allowed Bobby to recreate a scene from the book that was particularly meaningful to him. Some of the work on the project involved shaving bark from trees in the neighborhood. Jack, his father, worked with him on it. Jack used a knife to gather the bark, and he also helped with the general construction where it required tasks that were a bit too difficult or required skills with tools that were a bit unsafe for a young child.

When Bobby brought his project to school, he had it labeled with a card describing what it was and why he did it, and listing both his name and his father's. In doing so, he acknowledged that he had help. Several important things happened as a result of this acknowledgment. Bobby felt good about his part, he did not feel as if he were perpetrating a fraud on his teacher or his classmates, and he recognized his own limitations and generated a product of which he was very proud. Please understand that it is far more detrimental to take over and do a project for your child to get an A on it than it is for a child to do the work herself and get a B. Think about the message the child gets when a parent does the task. The hidden message is,

"You can't do it right." The more appropriate message is, "We can openly work and grow together."

Everyone responds to and thrives on praise, and children are no different. Parents are the most significant people in a child's life, and children value their opinions the most. Positive reinforcement, with such statements as, "Good first draft of the story!" or "I see how hard you're working on this assignment," works wonders. The feedback that you give your child must be honest. Children know when they haven't done their best work. You might try saying, "You worked so hard on this assignment and have so many good ideas, but maybe we can make them easier to understand." Be sure to then provide positive feedback on the revision.

For you as a parent concerned about your child's schooling, it is critical to continue to communicate with your child's teacher. Research shows that children who have involved parents do better in school. If you are a working parent, you can still be involved. Parent-teacher conferences are a small part of this two-way communication. Don't wait for them to be scheduled, though. Early on in the school year, make an appointment to meet with your child's teacher. If, because of your work schedule, this is too difficult, then make an appointment to have a phone conference, or use email or texting if that is possible. Informal chats during drop-off and pick-up times can do much to build relationships of trust between you and your child's teacher. If your child gets to school another way, then a brief note to the teacher helps. The important thing is for you and the teacher to have an open line of communication and for your child to know that you are interested, care about her school day, and are aware of the activities she is engaged in during the day.

It is important to monitor your child's progress through meetings, discussions, and reports from her teacher. It is also helpful and important to attend school events such as back-to-school night or open-house night, where teachers explain their programs. When there is time set aside for parent-teacher conferences, be sure to go and discuss your child's progress. If you have any questions, do not hesitate to ask. The more you and your child's teacher communicate, the better for your child. If you have concerns, you should share them with the teacher. If you think your child should be doing better, discuss this with the teacher. The teacher may allay your fears or may concur with you. Your school system may have access to special resources, such as a reading specialist or guidance counselor, to address your child's needs. In most cases, the teacher and principal will be able to shed light on your child's progress and what you might do to help. In addition, you may learn that your child is in fact doing fine and is progressing very well. As parents, we know that it is often hard to keep your child's progress in proper perspective, and speaking with your child's teacher may help.

If you can volunteer in your child's class, this is highly advantageous, even if it is only once or twice during the school year. Talk with your child's teacher about your expertise, interests, and availability. Good teachers welcome parents into their classrooms. If you feel you have no specific relevant expertise, then volunteer to go on a trip with the class or help organize the library or tutor a child. All too soon you will find that your child no longer wants you in her classroom, so enjoy the experience now! As we mentioned in the previous chapter, hopefully your child's school will have an active parent group that explores topics of interest to parents. If they do, then you should try to be involved in setting up some of the discussion topics.

Finally, since this book is about raising mature readers and writers, providing an atmosphere at home where your child sees you reading—whether it is a newspaper, a magazine, or a novel and writing is critical. Conversations you have with your child provide a foundation upon which to build as she grows. In doing so, you are showing her not only the value of reading and writing but the importance of thinking and sharing ideas with others.

A Focus on Reading and Writing

Proficiency in literacy comes through four stages; the first two, listening and speaking, are discussed extensively in chapters 2 and 3. The next two important stages focus on reading and writing, when the evolving reader and the mature reader are faced with the need to read longer stories, to read some stories independently, to respond in writing to what they have read, and to answer questions about a story or an informational piece of writing. Frequently children of this age also need not only to write about what they have read but to share it with others.

Children come to school excited about learning to read and write. Somehow, though, as they progress through the grades, that excitement tends to wane so that far too many children eventually come to view reading and writing as chores rather than as pleasurable activities. We believe that some educational systems may well be at fault. How can this possibly be? As the natural, communicative aspect of reading and writing moves into tasks that must be tested, pressure is often placed on children, with the sad result that reading becomes drudgery rather than a joyful experience, and what was once a fun activity degenerates all too often into one that creates tension and pressure.

We have conducted many formal and informal studies with children. In some, we asked children what reading meant to them. Children in the early grades usually responded with answers conveying their delight in reading and in learning to read. Children in the third grade and above, unfortunately, often responded with answers like the following:

- Reading is boring.
- Reading is filling out workbook pages.
- Reading is answering the teacher's questions.
- Reading is writing stuff about what I read.
- Reading is following along when someone reads out loud.
- Reading is copying stuff from the chalkboard.
- Reading is sitting with a partner and reading together.

Very rarely have we heard older children say that reading is fun to do or that "reading is when I sit alone with a book." As parents, we need to help children understand that reading can remain fun, as well as that by reading we learn many new things.

Children who have been exposed to a wide variety of reading materials will draw on it to help them write. It is crucial for them at this stage to see the connection between reading, writing, listening, and speaking and to understand that what they can say they can also write—that writing is just another form of communication. In addition to writing about what they have read, evolving readers and writers begin to write stories of their own, some of which may be based on experiences they have had, while others are purely imaginative. As your child brings home his stories, be sure to read them, or to listen attentively if he prefers to read them aloud. Show your interest by asking questions, making comments, and either placing the story on a bulletin board or starting a scrapbook of stories so that other members of the family can enjoy them too.

Reading becomes even more vital as children progress through the grades. While much of the work in the early grades involves them in the acquisition of reading and writing skills, as they move on, their ability to read will increasingly impact their learning of content-area subjects such as science or social studies. Often, in schools, subject-area materials are learned through the use of textbooks, which can mean that children who are not proficient readers may not be able to comprehend the subject matter fully. In such a case, reading the textbook with your child will help tremendously. Talk about the key ideas of a selection, and work together to find details that support the main ideas. It's often helpful to use diagrams called graphic organizers to facilitate this process.

The first one shown below is a very simple one that details what to do in the event of a fire. It was created by Seth and his mother after Seth read about home and family safety. For some children, seeing the ideas from the book in diagram format makes the content easier for them to understand and helps them to remember the main points and key ideas.

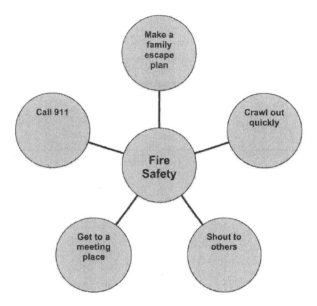

These next two graphic organizers were created by Carla after reading about healthy foods. In the first, Carla simply lists what types of foods are healthy. The second shows what Carla added after she and her father discussed different fruits and vegetables. Carla found that categorizing things can be a very helpful aid to understanding and remembering the ideas she reads about in a book.

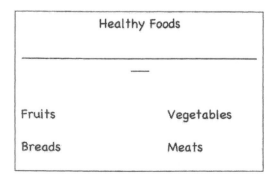

```
┌─────────────────────────────────────────────────┐
│                  Healthy Foods                    │
│  ───────────────────────────────────────────     │
│                      ──                           │
│                                                   │
│   Fruits                 Vegetables               │
│                                                   │
│   Apples                 String beans             │
│   Pears                  Peas                     │
│   Oranges                Carrots                   │
│   Peaches                Spinach                  │
│   Blueberries            Broccoli                 │
│   Strawberries           Cauliflower              │
│                                                   │
└─────────────────────────────────────────────────┘
```

Reading for Fun

Continue reading aloud to your child, even after she is reading on her own, because it fosters positive social interaction between you and her; she learns expression, increases her vocabulary, improves her listening skills, and, best of all, simply enjoys time alone with you. Reading aloud to her will help her develop positive attitudes about books, and it will stimulate her imagination.

Make reading time a priority. With busy schedules, it is easy for reading to get pushed aside in favor of other activities, but the value for your children is far outweighed by any inconveniences of scheduling. You might want to share this oral reading experience by having your child read parts of the book to you. Please remember that this is supposed to be the time for you to be the primary reader, but on occasion, let her chime in. In order to heighten both your own as well as her enjoyment, be sure to choose a book that you will both enjoy, as your enthusiasm for it will be transmitted to her. Be sure, too, to read the book first to yourself before you read it with her.

Select stories that have an interesting plot, frequent dialogue, some suspense and/or adventure, and suitable emotional content for the age and background of your child. Select those that are congruent with his interests. If he's experiencing a problem in his life, then you might want to select a book that deals with that problem. Children often work through issues in their lives through characters in books. The characters provide a safe haven for them to talk about their problems and ponder solutions.

Reading and enjoyment are promoted when the two of you engage in a book linked to an experience that helps your child understand the story or subject better. For instance, if you're reading *Molly's Pilgrim* by Barbara Cohen, you might decide to work together and make a rag doll that represents your heritage, or if you are reading *Cam Jansen and the Mystery of the Television Dog* by David A. Adler, or any other Cam Jansen mystery, you might chart out the clues and see where they lead. It is also helpful to set up a reading area in your home where you keep books that interest your child in a place where she can easily reach them when she wants to read independently. As she becomes a more proficient reader, make sure that you add books with more complex ideas to her collection.

As we have consistently affirmed throughout this book, be sure to demonstrate to your child that you are a reader too. Reading is a skill that is improved with practice. Research shows us that children who spend as little time as half an hour a day reading are much more likely to become good readers than those who don't spend any time at all doing it. Not an altogether surprising finding, perhaps, but do still try to set aside time when the entire family reads aloud or reads silently. Even if you can only squeeze in ten minutes, the benefits will still be substantial.

The love of literature can also be conveyed through the medium of audiobooks. You can listen to audiobooks instead of the radio on road trips or while traveling to and from activities, but please don't let this take time away from conversations with your child. Audiobooks, like the books you read to your child, can expose her to works that she is able to comprehend but is not yet able to read. The use of audiobooks can also introduce her to a wider variety of genres than she currently reads. More and more public libraries have collections of both audiobooks and books on CD. Go to the library together, and select books for an upcoming trip. You might also want to take out the companion text, which you can read together when you stop on the trip or when you return home.

The Reading Process

The process of reading is a threefold one. Before reading, during reading, and after reading are all critical stages. Within each stage, there are different things you can do to share and enrich the experience.

Before reading:
- Let your child decide on the book she wants to listen to or read.
- If you are reading to her, be sure you are both comfortable, and make sure she knows that this is her special time with you.
- Discuss what the book will be about based on the title. Prediction is a very important skill for readers to develop.

During reading:
- Pause to share thoughts on the story, such as likes and dislikes.
- If she is reading aloud to you, try to overlook the mistakes she makes. Keep in mind that this should be a relaxing and enjoyable experience and that she is practicing her reading.
- Offer help with a word she is having trouble with. Just tell her the word. She will learn from hearing and seeing the word.

After reading:
- Talk about the book or story. Ask some questions.
- Where and when does the story take place?
- What were the major events in the book?
- Did the book meet your expectations?

- What did you think about the way the characters solved the problem?
- How would you solve the same problem?

Opportunities for Using Language

Family activities that focus on talking, listening, reading, and writing all ensure that your children's school experiences will be enhanced. Activities such as keeping a family journal, reading the newspaper together, creating a board game, planning a trip, answering mail, shopping, and cooking all involve language. You can put notes in lunch boxes or leave notes around the house. Make sure these are fun things to read.

At this age, children should be encouraged to write thank-you notes, send birthday cards, or use email to keep in touch with friends and relatives.

Dear Daddy
Thank You for
getting Me The CD
Player. I Love it.
Love
made

Children love to get mail, so if you have friends or relatives who live in another city or who are on vacation, encourage them to mail postcards or short notes to your children. They can also send email or text messages, as these have the advantage of quicker response times.

Some readers and writers enjoy writing independently. Ginny, a seven-year-old, loves to write in her diary:

> Hello diary. Today was a very exciting day for me. I was very nervous about my first swimming lesson at the YMCA but I finally put my head underwater. I almost didn't go because I was really afraid of putting my head underwater and I only told Sue because shes my best friend. Now I am not so afraid and I am really happy that I did it.

Although Ginny usually uses her diary for her most private thoughts, this was an entry that she wanted to share with her mother. Her mother was both surprised and pleased. It gave them both an opportunity to speak a little about fears and how we conquer them.

You and your child can begin to write stories together. Choose a title, discuss ideas, and then take turns writing sentences that express both of your ideas. Remember that the primary goal is to get thoughts down on paper—not to have all the spelling and grammar correct. This should be a sharing rather than a competitive endeavor, so when the story is finished, share it with other family members.

Since so many busy families eat out or consume takeout food, you can use the menus or food lists for a fun reading and writing activity. Gather up menus, read them together, and then ask your child which dishes from the array of menus she likes best or which she thinks sound good. Together create your own "restaurant"; give it a fun name with a menu that you write together and that includes lots of different dishes, with rich descriptions of those dishes. You can also encourage categorization by then taking the menu items and placing them in categories. These can be the usual categories like appetizers and main dishes or meat, fish, and so on, or they can be organized based on the ethnic origin of the foods. This activity has an added advantage in that it also may help you home in on the foods your child prefers! If you are adventurous and have the time, you might also try to cook one or two dishes together for a special occasion.

Plan a party, and have your child write both a menu and a shopping list. Here is an example of a menu that Patty created when she and her mom decided to have a dessert part y. Notice, too, that although Patty is quite adept at spelling, some of the words were spelled incorrectly, but none of the "named" desserts were. This is another example of how environmental print plays a strong role in reading and writing.

Reading and writing go hand in hand. The more your child has pleasurable experiences with reading, the more helpful they will be to her acquisition of writing skills. One problem that children begin to encounter at this stage is handwriting; they often do much better when writing with a computer, since that takes the problem of letter formation out of the writing. So if you do have a computer, help your child to begin using a word processing program.

Help him see that writing is just another form of communication. Make sure that he sees you writing, even if it is just a grocery list. Encourage him to write his own lists. Make a memory book or a vacation book using photographs that he annotates. Write a dialogue journal with him. Even if you do it only occasionally, it will help to convey to him that writing is a form of talk written down.

Here are some other ideas:

- You can make a small crossword-puzzle game together. You can begin with clues such as "He is my father" or "The color of the sky." You can then move into more complex clues such as "A great place for a catch" or "A box with four sides." If you play Junior Scrabble with your child, you can then use the board as the template for your crossword game. After playing together, take the words you used and create a crossword replica with clues. See if other family members can join in and help complete the crossword puzzle.
- Use letter tiles from any game to scramble up letters and make words. Make sure that you make words that he will know, and then each of you can take turns using the word in a sentence. You can also use letter tiles to develop groupings of words that all begin with the same letter.
- Encourage him to expand his vocabulary by selecting a word for the day. This can be a new word that each of you tries to use at least three times during the day, or it can be a word that you both decide you cannot use, thus fostering language expansion. For example, if you rule out the word *said*

for the day, discuss synonyms for that word, such as *yelled*, *replied*, *discussed*, or *whispered*. The richness of using different words will expand both his speaking and his writing vocabularies.

- When you are driving or traveling, you can look for words together. You can simply look for words that start with the same sound, or you can look for words that fall into special categories, such as words about cars, descriptive words, or words that show feelings.
- Play "I'm thinking of..." a game in which one of you thinks of something and then the other guesses what that is based on various clues you provide.
- Ask him to describe events in his life. Talking about his experiences will help him think about them. Giving detailed descriptions and telling complete stories will also help him learn about how stories are written and what the stories mean.
- Develop lists of words. You can list silly-sounding words, rhyming words, long words, words that have more than one meaning, or words that relate to a particular topic. Not only will these lists help increase your child's vocabulary, but they will also enhance his ability to categorize things.
- When sorting laundry, talk to him about how you sort the laundry by placing dark clothes in one pile and whites in another. Let him help you with this. When you are putting clean clothes away, ask him to match socks or sort underwear by size.
- Invite him to hand you tools while you work on the car or make a minor repair around the house. Talk about the tools and their purpose. Talk about each chore as you complete it. Explain what you are doing and why. This is also important in another way in that he can learn how important these chores, repairs, or tasks are to the whole family.

Above all, the single most important thing parents can do is to talk with their child. Throughout any day there are many opportunities for short or extended conversations. Be sure to take advantage of them, whenever and wherever they may occur.

Going on Trips

Almost all families plan times to do special things together. Visiting family and friends, going on vacation, going to the park for a play-date, and taking a trip to the local zoo or children's museum are all opportunities for language learning. Conversations before the special event, lots of talk during the activity, and talking, drawing, or writing after the activity will make the experience more fun for everyone and provide opportunities for language to come alive for your child. Both local trips and longer trips provide many opportunities for teachable moments, as well as an opportunity to use the computer. The computer may be used to identify the local chamber of commerce in order to seek out sights they would like to visit. They can look for restaurant listings and help decide what restaurants you will all visit. When you go on a long trip, be sure to encourage them to write postcards and/or emails to friends and other family members. Bring along audiobooks. You might even select a book that might be a bit difficult for your child to read but that she can enjoy listening to. Talk about the audiobook as you would a print book, asking questions about the plot, the characters, the ending, and so on.

Vacations, even very short ones, involve planning, packing, looking at maps, and figuring out places to stay and things to eat. While the details noted below are primarily for longer trips, some of the ideas can be discussed as you talk about local trips. Children generally enjoy being part of a conversation that involves going somewhere away from home.

Planning

A part of planning is knowing the season of the year, the kind of weather to expect when you arrive at your destination, and the kind of transportation you will be using. While short trips tend to use a car, a bus, or a train, longer trips may use air travel or ship travel. Decide on the dates for the vacation and mark them off on the wall calendar. Your child is likely to ask questions such as, "How many days before we leave?" or "How many days will we be away?" These can lead to counting and reading the names of the days of the week. If you have a pet, will that pet be going along, or do you have to find someone to take care of it? As planning continues, there will be many opportunities to have conversations with everyone going on the trip so that their interests and ideas are included. This is the sort of activity that will engage you and your children in thoughtful discussions about plans that must be made.

Packing

Depending on the type of vacation and the amount of time away from home, your child can be involved in choosing what to pack. Talk about how the types of clothes that would be best to take for a summer vacation at the beach or a lake will be very different from those for a winter vacation that may be very cold and for which you may need to include heavy sweaters. This planning can also include a discussion of whether the family will be spending more time indoors or more time outdoors. This type of conversation will help children to decide on what kind of clothing, toys, and games to pack and how many items they will need to pack. For example, four jigsaw puzzles may be a good idea for a mostly cold and indoor vacation, whereas one puzzle may be sufficient for an outdoor summer vacation.

Looking at Maps

Even young children can be made aware of routes and places they will pass on the way to the final destination. Both automobile travel and air travel lend themselves to looking at maps. Although your young child will not be able to read all the various places on the map, she can see where you live and, by following your finger, how far away you are going. Trace out the route with your finger. Keep in mind that the scale of the map may be different from others you have used, and the travel distance may seem shorter or longer. What is important is that your child sees you using a variety of print materials as a part of your life.

Places to Stay

You can describe the kind of place where you will be staying. Is it the home of a family member or friend? A one- or two-story motel, or a high-rise hotel with an elevator? Does it have a pool for children? Is there a playground or swings? Will there be many other children there? If you have a brochure or can access pictures from a website, share them with your child. And, of course, encourage him to ask questions about the place. In this way, he will become more familiar with where you will be staying and more comfortable when you arrive.

Places to Eat

You can suggest to your child that she talk to everyone in the family who is going with you about their favorite foods. While she tells you what she's found out, you can make a list of everybody's favorite foods, with the name of the person who particularly likes that food next to each item. You and your child can generate this list and then talk about the kinds of eating places that offer these foods. You may also want to discuss the answers to one or more of the following questions: Will you be eating home-cooked food while staying with family or friends? Will you be shopping for your own food and cooking it in a rented apartment or cottage? Will you be eating mostly at fast-food places or sit-down restaurants?

While you are traveling, here are a few additional things to try:

- Word association games: You say a word, and your child says a word that relates to it.
- Play "Twenty Questions": Select something that is "animal, vegetable, or mineral," and have your child ask twenty questions in an effort to ascertain what that is.

- Play "Geography": Start with the name of a city or state. The next person must come up with a city or state that starts with the ending letter of the preceding one.
- Play "What if...": Come up with silly things such as, "What if a football were a round circle?"
- Make up silly songs, rhymes, jokes, or riddles.
- Tell or listen to family stories and memories of earlier trips.

Can't get away? Plan a fantasy vacation in which your child and you do the same planning as if you were going to a faraway place. Then spend a weekend as if you were in that place. Cook regional dishes, rent a video that takes place in that locale, read a travel magazine article about that area, or simply talk about what it would be like to be there.

Using Media

Television and Movies

The amount of television that your child watches depends entirely on you. It is important for parents to set some limits on television viewing because television can be a very passive medium and one that limits social interaction. Studies have indicated that children watch an average of twenty-eight hours of television a week—the equivalent of two days a week of waking time! Further, the American Academy of Pediatrics concluded that, by eighteen, the average American teenager would have spent more time watching television than being in school. In addition, they estimated that eighteen-year-olds would have watched almost four hundred thousand television commercials. Television fosters passivity in children, and many physicians feel that the alarming increase in childhood obesity is directly related to such passivity. These facts are offered merely to help you put television viewing into its proper perspective. What children watch and how often they watch television are extremely important considerations for today's parents and caregivers.

At this stage, children generally favor cartoons, sitcoms, or action-type shows and movies. The issue of violence in action shows is obviously a matter of grave concern for parents of children of all ages, and of course you'll want to be aware of what shows your child is watching. But television watching and moviegoing can be highly beneficial if they spark conversations and if they foster critical thinking. If you watch television or go to the movies with your child, be sure to talk about what you are watching, discussing the main idea of a show, the plot, the characters, and the sequence of the events that unfolded. Talk also about why a particular show is of interest, asking what your child liked best about the program. Compare the program with others the child enjoys. How is this show like those? In what ways is it different?

When you watch television with your child, you will often watch shows that have commercials. Evaluate with her the claims made for the products the sponsors are selling. What makes something "new and improved"? Is there any proof that a product works "better" or tastes "the best"? You can also turn this into an activity by actually testing the claims of some of the commercials.

It can be valuable to use something from television or the movies to connect with a book, since books, magazines, or comic books tied to popular TV shows or movies can spark a real interest in reading. Try to expand your child's interests so that television or movies have to compete with more active or interesting activities, such as building a model, creating a script, playing a sport, or going to a playground with friends.

Additional details on television viewing may be found in chapter 3, Your Preschool Child on pp.63-64.

Using Computers

Recent developments in computer software have resulted in programs that are very interactive, engaging, and informative. Software and apps geared toward children should be simple to use and have great graphics and plenty of information.

Like with any other purchase, be aware of claims that may be unfounded. As with all major purchases, you must do your homework! Read reviews and get only one or two programs to begin with. There are programs and apps geared toward all aspects of learning, but they should all include some element of exploration, imagination, or creativity. Be sure the instructions are developmentally appropriate for the age level for which it is designed. If your child is new to computers, look for programs that are simple and that only require the movement of the mouse or the click of a single button. Good software packages will involve many of the senses and have a variety of activities and levels of activities. Avoid any programs or apps that involve skill-and-drill activities or those that involve violence in any form. In earlier chapters, we cautioned parents about the use of computers with young children based on our conviction that, although children in grades two and three can benefit greatly from the use of computers, that does not mean that you should promptly go out and buy one for your child. Most schools and libraries have computers that children can use, and it may be possible for your child to use your computer for special assignments. With ever-changing technological advances, we suggest that you wait until your child is in middle school to purchase one for her. If you buy one now just for your child, you can be sure that by the time she is really in need of it, the one you bought will be obsolete. If, nevertheless, you are determined that you really *must* buy one for her, make sure to get one that is relatively inexpensive yet capable of handling appropriate software.

Computers will not make your child smarter, nor will they take the place of any of the parent-child activities we recommend. But children can learn by using computers properly, and it can be of benefit to some children. Nevertheless, as with books, children need opportunities to make their own choices about some of their computer experiences. Parents should always be on hand to guide and monitor their children's use of computers, and to offer help and advice when asked. Of course we cannot emphasize enough that, as in all media, you need to monitor and be aware of what your child is reading and doing.

While many parents are rightfully concerned about too much internet use, it is important to remember that the internet relies almost exclusively on reading. Computers are wonderful vehicles for both reading and writing. When children write drafts of stories using the computer, they very often are not as reluctant to write a second draft and revise their work for publication, since this becomes a relatively painless task. Also, children love to add clip art or pictures to their writing, and computers facilitate this.

Using the Library

Libraries today are different from the ones some of us remember. As in all aspects of your child's educational life, the library plays an important role in the development and enhancement of your child's literacy. It is a place to go for special events, such as listening to the librarian reading aloud or watching a special movie, or just to visit so your child can browse through many books before choosing one or more to take home. The value of these visits will be immeasurable as your child moves from being an evolving reader to a mature reader.

It also becomes an important resource if research on a school project is needed. It is a place where the young reader can have access to a computer and to the internet if a computer is unavailable at home. Also, family visits to the local public library provide an opportunity for you to use the adult books section, examine software, or listen to an audio tape while your child is busy either on the computer, listening to a story, or examining books. As a parent, you can provide an excellent model for your child when you show your interest in reading by borrowing a few books for yourself at the same time that she does.

In this chapter, we have discussed a number of issues that have an impact on the evolving reader and writer. It is at this stage that your child interacts on a regular basis with his parents, grandparents, caregivers, siblings, teachers, and friends. It is important to remember that as he grows, the level of his involvement changes, as school and friends become increasingly important. It is critical that as you and your child listen and speak to each other, read together, write together, and play together, you relax and enjoy to the fullest the wonderful and varied stages through which your child is progressing.

CHAPTER 6
MATURING READERS AND WRITERS

Ana and Juan are sitting at the dinner table on a Sunday evening and having a discussion about school homework. Both of their children, Marco, age ten, and Julie, age nine, are in their rooms watching television.

Ana: You know, Marco gets so much homework these days, he hardly has time to do anything that he really likes—not even reading a magazine. I don't think that is really good for him.

Juan: Oh, some work won't hurt him. He'll have plenty of time to read what he wants when he's older.

Ana: I disagree. He used to enjoy reading, but now all he reads is what he has to. I noticed that some of his homework is just busywork, like copying the answers to questions in his social studies book. It wouldn't be so bad if he at least had to look up the answers on the computer or in another book.

Juan: What about Julie? I don't see that she has a lot of homework.

Ana: Well, Julie's only in fourth grade, but even she's starting to complain. She wanted to play some games on the computer, and I told her she had to finish all her homework first. By the time she finished, it was time for bed, and she was really unhappy. I think it's time we found out if the school has a policy on homework—you know, how much each night and if they get one night off.

Ana and Juan have every reason to be concerned. The artificial imposition of homework can result in situations in which students are given assignments that are not truly extensions of their learning but rather take the form of worksheets and tasks given just to take up time. The issue of homework has many layers. Should children always be assigned homework? How much is too much? What types of homework are beneficial? Should parents help children with their homework? The topic of homework will be discussed in detail in chapter 7, Special Topics.

This chapter focuses on the important middle school years when children are becoming independent readers and writers. During these years, reading and writing are crucial skills as children learn new information from fields such as science and social studies. At this critical juncture in their children's educational journey, parents should continue to be strongly supportive of their children's learning, as well as knowledgeable about the school's expectations.

Here are some questions to think about as you read this chapter:
- How does my middle school child deal with her world?
- What is an appropriate level of parental involvement during these years?
- What is the school's focus on reading and writing for this age group?
- How do computers and television influence my child?
- What are the issues surrounding homework?
- How does the stress of school tests affect my child?

The Mature Reader and Writer

The middle grade child is going through many physical, emotional, and educational changes, often all occurring at the same time! While these changes occur for different children at different times, they do appear to follow a common time line. Young adolescent learners often can't sit still, and while they are extremely social, they are basically insecure. They desire routines and structure yet have a need to demonstrate independence. They like to argue and debate, are very curious, are active rather than passive learners, and relate to real-life problems and situations. The following brief conversation depicts a typical early adolescent's behavioral dichotomy. Bonnie (speaking to her mom): "Can't you just leave me alone? I hate you." After about an hour, Bonnie said, "Can you take me to the mall this afternoon?"

It's often hard for parents to not personalize their child's angry comments. We need to understand that she is conflicted about who she is, what she wants, and how to get there. Part of what the middle school child struggles with are the demands of school, friends, and family. Too often one aspect dominates the others, and the child does not know how to "get out from under it." She may often seem confused and have difficulty deciding what is most important. To adults, the priorities seem simple, but to a nine- or ten-year-old, it is all extremely baffling. If your child is like most, her room is in total disarray, with clothes strewn all over and drawers half-open with socks and T-shirts hanging out. The room often reflects her mind. This chaos, this attempt to organize and make sense of the world, is difficult. As parents, we want to guide our children through the process of juggling the demands of school and friends, while at the same time fostering the child's natural desire to read and write.

Perhaps the easiest and most important thing you can do is to show keen interest in what your child is doing. If in response to the question, "What did you do in school today?" you get the usual, "Nothing much," then it's time for you to probe a bit and ask specific questions. The purpose is twofold: to learn about what's going on in school and to show that you are interested in what happens to your child when he is at school. Even though some children during these middle grade years seem to want us uninvolved, they ultimately will respect, admire, and enjoy such care and concern. With proper motivation, guidance, and encouragement, your child will see education, and specifically literacy, as significant and enjoyable aspects of his life.

The Role of Parents

It is important that your child sees you as an integral partner in her education. Parents, whether we work inside or outside the home, can form partnerships with schools. Our involvement may take varied forms, depending on our time constraints, work schedule, and multiple responsibilities. In the ideal situation, we would all have plenty of extra time to spend helping out in our children's school, but if you are like most parents today, you are often extremely busy, either with work or family responsibilities, so your involvement may of necessity take different forms.

For example, we often look forward to relaxing on weekends. These relaxing times, however, can on occasion be ruined by homework battles. In order to preserve weekend leisure time and at the same time foster good management skills, develop a family planning time on Friday evening in which all members of the family indicate the "work" they need to do and allot specified times in which the work can be done. If you have to rake the leaves, your child might use that time to write a report, send a letter to a friend, study, or practice his part in a school play. Your child will be less resistant to doing homework when he sees that you, too, are doing your "homework." Slotting these special times will also free up everyone to have specific fun time, without the tension and worry that often accompany weekend assignments.

One important thing is that we keep track of what our children are doing in school. In order to accomplish this, visit the school, observe classes, and talk to your child's teacher. Although parent-teacher conferences typically occur two times per year on a formalized basis, it is important to realize that such formal meeting times are often insufficient. Parent-teacher conferences can be a source of either apprehension or joy for parents. In order to alleviate any possible apprehension, it might help to remember that all parties in this interaction share the common goal of wanting to help your child learn effectively and socialize in a positive manner. Before going to the conference, ask your child if she has any questions or concerns that she would like you to discuss with her teacher. Think about what you'd like to learn from the conference, and also review the things you'd like to share with your child's teacher.

It is important to realize that the formalized twice-yearly meetings present a real time crunch for both you and the teacher. The following hints may help you use that time effectively:

- Be realistic and remember that your child has strengths and weaknesses.
- Be honest and share your concerns.
- Come prepared with specific questions.
- Be an active listener.
- Take notes.

Some things you might want to discuss include the following:

- Particular concerns about your child's academic progress or social progress.
- Problems that you may be having at home regarding homework.
- Clarification of some aspect of the curriculum or of some specific long-term assignments.
- External family matters that may be impacting your child's performance.

While these school-wide meetings are scheduled infrequently, you should not be limited by them. Most teachers welcome contact with parents, either through further face-to-face meetings, through phone conversations or email, or through notes. Parents have a right and an obligation to stay in close contact with the school, so make sure that the teacher has a way of contacting you. If you need to call a teacher, do so early in the morning so that he can return the call later on in the day. If there are specific times that you can or cannot be reached, leave word, but remember that during the school day, a teacher often has strict time constraints on his ability to leave the classroom. Generally it is preferable to use email or a text message if you know that the teacher has a mobile phone or computer so that she can respond to you at an appropriate time.

While helping children to become independent readers and writers is primarily the role of the school during the middle grades, there are still some things that you as a parent can do outside school. Children of this age are beginning to focus on their peers as role models, and it is in this area that you can make an impact. Parents can be instrumental in forming groups in which their children can participate with their friends. Among the activities are planning for a group trip, setting up an after-school or summer reading group, starting a neighborhood newspaper, or selecting a preschool to visit, with the idea that each middle school–aged child would talk and/or read to a younger child. Another idea is to start a community project in which middle school children read stories aloud on tape that will be sent to visually disabled children. While some of these activities may require school cooperation, many of them can be started by a group of concerned parents. And these activities, in which your child will interact with his peers in a nonschool setting, all involve talking, listening, writing, and reading. Through such outside-of-school experiences, many children develop a lifelong love of reading and writing while at the same time developing important friendships.

But above all, please remember that involvement in your child's education may take many forms. We can show our commitment by looking at homework, collaborating on school projects, getting involved in community activities, encouraging other family members or caregivers to take an active role, and simply asking our children to talk about their school experiences.

A Focus on Reading and Writing

For the student in the middle grades, reading and writing are the building blocks of learning. Whether she is listening to you read, reading and writing independently at home, or reading and writing in school, these activities are important ways for her to expand her knowledge about the world.

Reading Together

Previously, we have talked quite a bit about the importance of reading aloud. This holds true even as your child progresses through the middle grades. Reading a chapter book aloud each night is still an excellent idea. Just read one chapter, particularly if the book is a mystery. It is even possible that your child will want to read the next chapter to you. If time is short, you might read a joke or an editorial or a sentence that really struck you. Encourage your child to find an interesting article, picture, or advertisement from the newspaper. Take turns reading something in the newspaper, possibly a news article, or even the comics. Talk about what you have read, and be sure to ask your children for their thoughts about the events. This kind of experience sets the stage for the importance of reading and talking about the material that has been read. Help your child see that reading is important by exposing her to a wide variety of reading materials, such as newspapers, books, catalogs, recipes, cartoons, television listings, crossword puzzles, games, and magazines.

Setting aside a special time in which you and your child read is important, even if it is only ten or fifteen minutes. We all lead such busy lives, and we know how hard it is to find spare time, but ten minutes or so really won't make a great difference to us, and it ultimately will have a significant beneficial effect on your child. Besides, wouldn't we all want to have the luxury of taking some time to read and relax with a book? In some families, this special time is after dinner or just before bedtime. It is very important that you and your child mutually agree on the best time of day to spend together.

Independent Reading

Emma, a fifth grader, is very interested in reading about scientific topics. She has just finished reading about the environment. She was particularly interested in things that are polluting our planet. As a follow-up to her reading, she decided to divide pollutants into two categories: those you could see and those you could hear.

Here is the chart prepared by Emma:

Things That Pollute the Environment

Visual Pollutants	Auditory Pollutants
Dog droppings	Loud car horns
Billboards	Trucks backfiring
Garbage in the street	Loud radios
Empty shopping carts near our apartment building	People yelling
	Dogs barking

Emma brought this chart home and was able to explain to her mother that some of the things she listed were personal pollutants that might well not bother everyone. Clearly, she understood the material that she had read and the concept of classifying things into categories.

In contrast to Emma, there are some children who have a negative attitude toward reading almost anything.

Tomas: I hate to read. Reading is a stupid thing. I spend so much time reading things for school that mean nothing to me.

Father:	What is it about you, don't you know that reading is important?
Mother:	When I was your age, I would read all the time.
Tomas:	Things were different then; you didn't have much else to do. My teacher assigns such boring things, and it's so hard for me. I never remember what I read.

This brief scenario depicts the plight of some school students. Too often they find reading a chore rather than an enjoyable act. Multiple interests and activities compete with reading as a pleasurable activity. Too many children at this age don't find books that are particularly relevant to their lives.

The most important thing we can do is to listen to our children, paying particular attention to their successes and their problems. We need to acknowledge that they may, at this age, have interests that to them take precedence over anything related to school. We can help them find books that they can relate to their lives. By acknowledging their interests and not negating them, we can help our children open up to a world in which computers, sports, music, art, and other hobbies compete with each other for their time. Capitalizing on our children's interests is the key if we want to encourage them to read and write independently. Tomas's parents can help him by first recognizing that reading is difficult for him but also by helping him to find books that spark his interest. Tomas loves basketball, and when he reads a story built around that theme, his interest helps him handle the difficulties that he sometimes encounters in the text.

The idea of comfort is crucial. It is far better for children to read books that are comfortable but perhaps a bit easy for them than to struggle reading a book that is too hard. This is especially true for those children for whom reading is not an easy task.

Think about the following situation. When Janey was about nine years old, all her friends started to go ice skating, and Janey went with them. While they spun around the ice, Janey struggled just to keep her ankles straight. But try as she might, her ankles always turned in. Week after week they went to the ice rink, and even though Janey got better, she still couldn't enjoy it. It was work and it wasn't fun. After a while, Janey stopped ice skating. Luckily, ice skating was not a necessary part of her life. She could easily become a successful adult without ever going on the ice again.

But let's think about substituting the concept of reading for ice skating. Our children can't opt out of reading and writing. It is an integral part of their lives. But often, both in school and at home, children are confronted with feelings like those Janey felt when on the ice. Most of us do not want to do something that we are not good at or from which we do not derive a sense of success or pleasure. Try to find activities that you know your children will find both fun and interesting. Taking our children to the library, the bookstore, and local stores can provide many enjoyable experiences that involve language.

The following are some of the things to keep in mind as you guide your children to books with which they can connect and that they can enjoy:

- What are his interests, hobbies, or special talents?
- Does he enjoy sports, fantasy, history, or adventure?
- What types of movies or television shows does he watch most frequently?
- What types of video games does he favor?
- Does he shun books with sad endings?
- What books seem "comfortable" for him?

If your child sees that reading and writing are valued and pleasurable activities for you, then you are establishing the model for him. Share your enjoyment of something you have just read, or ask him to help you write a shopping list before the two of you go shopping. Talk to your child about a book you would like to read or one you've read and didn't like. Also, talk about the fact that sometimes you don't finish a book because it was not interesting, and that is an OK thing to do.

The following conversation between Lina, age nine, and her mom describes a parent who is a "model" for her daughter:

Mom: Lina, I'm going to the bookstore to look for some books. Would you like to come with me?

Lina: Mom, I thought you bought two books a few weeks ago. Did you finish them already?

Mom: No, one of them was great. I had trouble putting it down. The author really made the characters come to life. I felt as if they were real. The author got me interested in what was happening to the characters. I tried to solve the crime, but there were so many twists and turns, I couldn't. It was a mystery, and it was a real page-turner.

Lina: So you still have the other book.

Mom: Yes, I know, but I just can't seem to get interested in it. This one takes place hundreds of years ago, and I'm not enjoying it very much. It got great reviews, so I bought it. I think I made a mistake. I've read about three chapters, and I really can't get into it, so I have stopped reading it. I may give it to a friend of mine who I know enjoys stories that take place a long time ago.

Lina: Yeah, I know what you mean. Sometimes when I have to find a book to read for school, it takes me a long time. Sometimes in silent reading time, my teacher even gets angry because we spend so much time picking our books that we don't have much time to read.

Mom: How do you find books that you like?

Lina: Usually if Gina recommends a book, I like it too. She and I like the same characters.

Mom: Me too. I have never been disappointed in any book that Judy recommends to me.
Lina: You know, Mom, I think I'll go with you. Maybe I'll find something that Gina and I will like.

Lina is lucky to have a parent who shares not only her reading "successes" but also the notion that it's okay to start a book and decide that it isn't one you particularly want to finish. Lina's mother opened a dialogue in which they relate to each other as readers. This kind of dialogue is crucial as we try to foster a love of reading in our children. We need to respect them as readers and value their ability to make choices.

Encouraging Writing

Joshua, a fourth grader, enjoyed reading poetry and decided to participate in a Valentine's Day poetry contest at his school. Here is the poem that he wrote and brought home to share with his younger sister, Anita, age six. She was so pleased that her brother had written a poem for her that she had him read it to her over and over again. Soon Anita was able to read it with him, and eventually she could read it on her own.

Teddy Bear

A present for my baby sister
Warm as a fur coat
Softer than a fluffy kitten
Unlike a real bear with rough
skin and a temper
He never gets angry
A very quiet thing
Always happy and smiling
He never criticizes when I have
a problem
He makes me feel warm and good

Happy as a person with every
thing they wanted
I can see him
Sitting with arms open
Waiting for me to get into
bed and hug him

There is a clear connection between reading and writing. The two go hand in hand. It is important to expose children to a wide variety of reading materials, as this benefits not only their reading but also their writing. Children often emulate the writing styles they see in books. Writing is also a forum in which children crystallize their ideas and thoughts; it helps them focus and make concrete connections. Before discussing ways to encourage writing at home, we think it is important for you to be knowledgeable about how writing is generally taught in schools.

In a structured writing program, children will be encouraged to write on topics of interest to them. The first step is referred to as a first draft and will be revised. Both the teacher and other children have input into this first draft, with the goal of improving the writing. Children in small groups may listen to this first draft and offer their comments.

Comments such as the following are helpful to the writer:
- "I didn't understand that sentence. Can you explain what you mean?"
- "I liked that paragraph, but could you add something about ____?"
- "Here's a word that I think would really help me to picture what you are saying." (Student gives classmate a word.)
- "There's too much stuff near the end. Could you leave some of it out?"

All of the comments from both the teacher and fellow students then lead to a second or even a third draft. The final stage in a writing program is a final draft, with the idea being a goal of publication. Publication may mean a classroom-initiated book consisting of student writings, a school bulletin board, or a school-wide publication. In some schools, student writing is published in parent newsletters or as material to be read by students in the lower grades.

Here is an example of a first draft written by Beth, a fourth grader, after reading the story *Jumanji* by Chris Van Allsburg. In this story, a game is played by rolling the dice, and depending on where the dice land, a real event occurs—some scary! Yelling "Jumanji!" causes the event to go away. Beth decided to write her own adventure.

(Beth)

Quicksand

rolled Judy cautiosly a 4 on the dice. She moved her piece to the 4th square. She landed on a square that said "Quicksaid." Judy reached down to tie her shoe lace and all of the sudden her left foot started sinking. All of a sudden Peter started saying dun da dun da dun. Judy said roll the dice Peter. Peter rolled the dice and got a 3 he landed on a blank space all th quicksand disappeared with every thing else!

Here is the final draft of "Quicksand" after Beth heard comments from both fellow students who had read *Jumanji* and her teacher. The final draft was done on a classroom computer and published in the fourth grade newspaper.

Quicksand

by Beth Chin

Judy cautiously rolled a 4 on the dice and moved her piece to the 4th square. She landed on a square that said, "Quicksand." Judy reached down to tie her shoelace and all of a sudden her left foot started sinking. She looked down. There was quicksand everywhere. She yelled, "Jumanji!" but nothing happened. She yelled again and nothing happened. Her friend Peter was playing the game with her. Peter started saying, "dum, da dum, da dum." Judy yelled, "HELP! Roll the dice Peter, my foot is going deeper." Peter rolled the dice and got a 3. He landed on a blank space and all of the quicksand disappeared along with everything else.

You will note that in Beth's final draft above, she has expanded on her first draft and uses all the conventions of the English language. As a parent, you may very well read many first drafts of your child's writing as she moves up the grades. Your concern should be about the ideas expressed and not about the correct punctuation and grammar, as these things will be improved in any work that is "published." Remember, a lot of first-draft writing is used to express ideas and may never be published. As children become mature readers and writers, they may decide to send first and second drafts of their writing in a document to friends who will respond with comments and suggestions for changes. In this way, children can often get quick responses from others before writing final drafts for school-related writing assignments.

In addition to praising and encouraging your child's school writing, there are several fun activities you can share with your child to encourage her to write. Try, for example, writing a family cookbook, with anecdotes about particular dishes or traditions. One family gathered such anecdotes, and the children were delighted to find out stories such as the time grandma left a sponge in the meatloaf, or the time the sweet potato pudding fell all over the floor. Writing these anecdotes not only encourages children's writing but also helps preserve precious memories and forge close intergenerational ties.

Another project you and your child can do together is to go on a photo expedition or to select some family photos from a previous outing to create a book of photo essays or notations for the pictures. The essays or notations can be simple or complex, depending on the motivation for the project and your child's ability. If you or your child is technologically advanced, you might scan the pictures and the text into a computer and create a digitized collection. Encourage other family members to read the book and write their own reactions or reflections.

Many children of this age begin to keep a diary. Here is a place for their private thoughts, fears, ideas, and just musings. Here is a writing and reading activity that is self-initiated and important. As a parent, remember to respect the privacy of these communications, and do not ask to share them. Of course, if your child chooses to read some part to you, then you can show the appropriate interest.

If you work outside the home and have email access both at work and at home, send a message to your child each day. Email is a beneficial means of communicating because it sets up clear connections between thinking, reading, and writing. This quick communication from you provides him with something special to look forward to and also conveys the importance of reading and writing. However, don't necessarily expect a response to each of your messages.

While many parents believe that their children spend too much time on the computer, one must realize that much of what they are doing involves lots of reading and writing. It is an excellent tool for finding information about many topics. Encourage your children to use the computer and the internet both for school-related assignments, at-home projects, and for their personal communications.

Going on Trips

Children of all ages—from the preschool child aged four to five years, to evolving and mature readers and writers—enjoy a short outing or a longer vacation with family and/or friends. Instead of including this topic in every chapter, we have discussed short trips and longer vacations in detail in chapter 5, Evolving Readers and Writers. Please select from the content in that chapter those activities that are most applicable to the age and developmental level of your child.

Science and History

In the middle school years, reading and writing begin to focus on topics in the areas of science and history. For parents, there are any number of ways that you can interest your child in these areas. Science is all around us, while today's newspaper headlines and television programs are tomorrow's history. By increasing your child's interest in science and history, you will be helping him to expand his vocabulary and extend and enrich his background information. Both of these will serve him well when he is expected to read and understand scientific information and historical concepts in textbooks.

A simple way to spark interest in science is to talk about the everyday things that we all encounter that have a scientific basis. For example, the weather is usually a topic of interest to children. The occurrence of thunderstorms, hurricanes, tornadoes, wildfires, and earthquakes can all lead to a discussion of the causes of these events. For some children, the moon, the stars, and the planets are of enormous interest. Just looking at the sky on a clear night can be the starting point for an in-depth conversation followed by some research. It is the perfect moment to visit a planetarium if one is located near you. If not, it is a good opportunity for the two of you to study the night sky with a star chart. Providing opportunities for your child to spend time with relatives, friends, or neighbors who work in fields other than yours can, of course, be invaluable. A visit to a laboratory, a hospital, or an automobile factory can lead to sustained interests and even thoughts about an eventual career.

Another topic that may be of interest to your child is animal life. Conversations about household pets, local animals, birds, and endangered species can include the eating, sleeping, and mating patterns of specific animals. Most local zoos now provide a wealth of information about each of the animals on view, and many of these animals are displayed within their natural habitat so their patterns of behavior can easily be seen and discussed. In addition, television programs such as those viewed on the Discovery Channel and Animal Planet focus on animal behavior, and viewing either of these channels will expand your child's concepts and vocabulary.

History is occurring every day. The daily newspaper and news programs on television and the internet are excellent sources of information about what is happening both locally and around the world. Discussions that emphasize the background of these events can lead to a clearer and better understanding of why something is happening today. The holidays that we celebrate are good jumping-off points for conversations about our past. President's Day, which commemorates both Washington's and Lincoln's birthdays, is a good time to talk about our first and sixteenth presidents and the times in which they lived. In the same way, Martin Luther King Day can lead to a conversation about the Civil Rights era. Memorial Day, Independence Day, and Labor Day all give us the opportunity to talk about and reflect on historical events.

Some children are interested in stamps and collect them as a hobby. Stamps frequently portray people of historical significance, so here is an opportunity to note the figure that is depicted and try to find out something about him or her. Why was this person important enough to deserve a stamp? Although we rarely look at our paper money and think about the person on it, your child may be interested in finding out why Jefferson, Lincoln, and Hamilton, among others, are pictured on our money. What did they do that was special in the history of our country? How is a historical person selected to be represented on our paper money?

Frequently, a newspaper article or television program that includes scientific or historical facts will lead your child to want more information, and this provides you with your cue to several activities. Among the things you can do are visiting the library and looking for books on the topic of interest. If possible, a visit to a science or natural history museum is an excellent way not only to spark interest in a topic but to expand existing knowledge and interest. Some museums have hands-on exhibits designed especially for children, as well as films that may be of special interest to your child. The History Channel and special television shows featuring the biographies of important people in history are good sources of information, along with, of course, research on the internet.

Using Media

Television and Movies
Television and movies in and of themselves are not necessarily detrimental to the literacy development of children. Problems sometimes arise if there is an abuse of the medium, resulting in children becoming mere passive viewers, or when they simply spend too much time watching television or movies. Limiting the amount of time your child spends watching television will enable her to discover many new vistas. On the other hand, selectively watching television or a movie with your child can also become an activity in which you both use the experience to build strong literacy skills.

For a start, read the television and movie listings in your local paper with your child. Talk about what you might enjoy watching together or independently. This is a good way to increase your awareness of what interests your child. Decide whether to read a write-up in the newspaper, a review of a show, an advertisement, or just a synopsis. Talk about the purpose of reviews and advertisements. Look at some of the vocabulary within advertisements, and discuss the words or phrases that are used to persuade people. After watching a show together, ask your child what he thought of the show. What did he find interesting? Were the events portrayed realistic? What were some of the character traits that your child found admirable? Were there flaws in any of the characters? Talk about other possible endings for the show. Try to use words like *plot*, *setting*, *characters*, *conflict*, *resolution*, and *conclusion* that will help your child to understand these concepts better when he is reading a story. You might also engage in a conversation about the tools that the author and/or directors used to convey their message, be it comedic, sad, poignant, mysterious, or just plain scary. Finally, encourage him to write about movies or television programs he sees, possibly a review that can be shared with family members.

Here are some additional ideas to use as you and your children watch television:

- Compare the news on television with what you read in the newspaper.
- Talk about why particular stories are "lead" stories.
- Discuss the differences between local, regional, national, and international news.
- Listen for biases in reporting.
- Talk about reporting versus opinion writing.
- Check the weather forecast in the newspaper, comparing it with what the television weatherperson reports.
- Tally the number of times a particular commercial is repeated.
- Chart the accuracy of the weather predictors by making a graph or chart.
- Note the use of descriptive language in commercials, such as "best," "superior," "gorgeous," "fastest," or "biggest."

- Listen for a word that is not in your child's vocabulary. Try to use it together throughout the day.

In school, children are often asked to find the main idea of a story and the supporting details. One of the easiest ways you can foster this skill is by modeling this task as you watch a dramatic show or a movie. Talk with your child about what you would put down if you were in charge of writing a television or movie listing. Ask your child to join you in developing your own synopsis of the shows or movies. Realizing that space limitations are placed on these listings, you might want to limit them to one or two sentences. Compare what you've said or written to that which is in the guide or newspaper. Talk about the differences and the similarities. The one or two sentences you decide upon are the main ideas of the show.

Using the Computer

If your child has his own computer at home, you know that he is spending time playing games and surfing the internet. Look at the kinds of games your child enjoys, and you'll gain insight into the kinds of books he might like. Much has been written about the potential dangers of children using the computer without any supervision or parental screening, and we'll add our own voice to the chorus of those decrying these practices. But using the internet properly can be a very useful tool for enhancing your child's learning. One obvious point which we must stress is that when surfing the internet, children are engaged in lots of reading and writing activities. For the internet to be productive, your child must know how to read and write and be able to select key words to input into search engines. The computer, a laptop, or a tablet can be used for research, for accessing information about authors, for recipes, for travel, and for general fun, as well as for communicating with friends and family.

One of the most valuable things we can do is to help our children become effective consumers of information. This applies not only to computer usage but to whenever they are confronted with any type of information. It becomes even more essential, however, when using the internet to access information, since there are very few limits, constraints, or review processes for what can be posted. Almost anyone with basic technological ability can post information. The task of discerning the truth of such information falls solely on the reader, and given these circumstances, we must encourage our children to be careful and cautious users of the information put forth. We can help them to find multiple sources of information on the same topic in order to determine the accuracy of the information. Whenever possible, children need to be able to discern the potential biases of the writers and to judge whether or not the information is factual. This is not an easy task, and as adults, we need to be available to answer our children's questions.

In this chapter, we have explored some of the important issues confronting children during their middle school years as they become mature readers and writers. As you discuss some of these issues with your child, you will note that some topics acquire greater prominence during these early adolescent years than others. Your child is in the process of formulating her personal identity, and you are an integral partner in that process.

CHAPTER 7

SPECIAL TOPICS

There are four topics that cut across several of the stages discussed in the previous chapters. Among these are homework issues, the emphasis on standardized testing, some ways of using technology for personal communication, and some ideas if your child needs help with reading and writing. Each of these topics may arise in one or more of the developmental levels previously discussed, but this chapter will focus on the commonalities inherent in each topic regardless of the age of your child.

Homework Issues

For as long as homework has been a part of school life in this country, so, too, has been the debate over its value. Parents are some of homework's most ardent supporters, and they are also its most vocal critics. The debate over homework often spills onto the pages of local newspapers and magazines, with calls to either abolish homework completely or to support it as a valuable after-school activity. As we know all too well, there are often situations where the demands of school, homework, and the pressures of formal or informal after-school activities interfere with the natural inquisitiveness and initiative of children.

Homework should be a natural extension of the school day and not be given just for the sake of giving homework. It should not consist of mindless tasks that are designed for the sole purpose of rote learning or repetition. Homework should engage your child in thinking deeply and broadly about what was learned in class. Districts, schools, and teachers should ensure that the total amount of homework students receive does not exceed the ten-minute rule. Educators agree that no more than ten minutes of homework multiplied by the student's grade level should be assigned. For example, a third grader would be assigned no more than thirty minutes, whereas a sixth grader could be assigned sixty minutes, or an hour, of homework. Too much homework may be an unnecessary burden on both students and parents.

As a parent who is concerned with your child's learning, it may be critical to discuss both the homework policy in your child's school and the type of homework assignments that are generally given. It strikes us that an arbitrary policy is not beneficial and that there should be a relationship between the type of homework assigned and the amount of time needed to complete it. Excellent opportunities for such a discussion are at open-school week, at a parent-teacher conference, or at a general meeting of parents, teachers, and administrators.

Homework assignments can vary greatly, as described by Ari and Jill in conversations with their parents below.

Arnold (father): What kind of homework do you have?

Ari (age 10): I have to finish reading this book and then fill out a book response sheet.

Arnold: What's on the response sheet?

Ari: The same questions we get after we read every book. I have to fill in the name of the book, the author, the number of pages, a list of the main characters, and a summary of the book. It's so boring.

Ari's voice is clear. This homework assignment does nothing to extend or enrich the reading experience. It appears to be an assignment that is merely given for the sake of checking to see if the reading was done. An assignment such as this does not engage the reader; even less does it make reading a book an enjoyable activity. Ari is just doing busywork.

In contrast, consider the following conversation:

Lee Ann (mother): What homework do you have today?

Pedro (age 11): I have to do a reading assignment. I have to imagine that I was the main character in the book I just finished, and I have to write what I would have done in his situation. I'm not sure what he did was right, but I'm not sure that he had any choice.

Lee Ann: What was it that he did?

Pedro: Well, he was hungry, so he took something to eat. He stole it, but I'm not sure that he was wrong. If you're starving, shouldn't you find food?

Lee Ann: I see your point, but what else could he have done?

Pedro: I guess he could have gone to someone for help, or he might have told an adult what was going on in his life.

This assignment is in sharp contrast to the one in which Ari was simply required to fill out a response sheet. Pedro's assignment actively engages him in the reading experience. He becomes a "participant" in the book as he grapples with different possibilities. He also begins to explore his own values and his family's values as they collaboratively discuss the effect of potential acts by the main character. This can become a family dinnertime discussion. It also becomes another time in which family members discuss their values and opinions. When Pedro sits down to write his reaction to the book, he will be using his own ideas, whereas Ari's teacher has not encouraged him to go beyond the book and really hasn't a clue as to what Ari himself thinks of the story and its characters.

It is important to note that children like to do their work in different physical spaces, and insisting that your child sit at a desk or table may not be beneficial. Look at the following scenario.

Rosa, age eight, comes home from school, and after she has a snack, her mom, Erica, tells her to go to her room and do her homework. Rosa trudges off to her room and dawdles before she starts. An hour later Erica goes in to check on her, and she discovers that Rosa is lying down on the floor, doing her work. Erica insists that Rosa go back to her desk to complete the work. An argument ensues and ends up with Erica being angry and Rosa crying and saying that she hates homework. This struggle seems to go on daily. Erica does not understand why Rosa won't just sit at her desk and do her work.

A few weeks later, Erica, having thought about the situation, tells Rosa that she can do her homework anywhere she wants, as long as it gets done. Rosa proceeds to lie on the floor in the middle of the house, near the kitchen, in what is the busiest area. Rosa's three-year-old brother is playing with his trucks and making traffic noises, and Erica is cooking, with pots clattering, but Rosa is doing her work.

What we have just described has elements that ring true in so many homes. Many of us were taught that there is a specific time, place, and way to do our work. However, knowledge of how people learn has made us realize that children have varying learning styles and preferences and that often, when left to their own devices, they will find the most natural, comfortable places and ways to do their work. There is no right or wrong. Some children will feel perfectly fine working at a desk, while others will not. Allow your child the opportunity to find her own way.

There are some things you as a parent can do to ease the problems associated with homework. One is to initiate a "homework organizer" program. To begin with, have a discussion with your child about any problems she may be having with homework and what can be done to make her life easier. Among the points that might come up are the following:

- Encouraging your child to have a homework partner. Your child and her partner can remind each other to bring the relevant books and supplies to and from school, discuss homework when an assignment is not clear, and generally keep in touch via phone, email, or text messages.
- Having a separate family calendar with adequate space for your child to write in long-term assignments and those assignments which may require assistance from family members.
- Encouraging your child to have one place in which to keep all the assigned tasks.
- Deciding where in the house your child prefers to do her assignments.
- Keeping abreast of the school's and each teacher's homework policy.

Given the controversy long surrounding the issue of homework, in late spring 2018, the Center for American Progress conducted an online survey investigating the quality of students' homework. The survey sought to better understand the nature of homework, as well as whether the homework assigned was aligned to rigorous academic standards.

The three key findings from the CAP survey are as follows:
- Homework is largely aligned to the Common Core standards.
- Homework is often focused on low-level skills in the Common Core standards, particularly in the earlier grades.
- Homework frequently fails to challenge students.

Based on these key findings, the Center for American Progress recommended the following:
- Schools and districts should develop homework policies that emphasize strategic, rigorous homework.
- Districts and schools should periodically audit homework to make sure it is challenging and aligned to standards.

- Schools and districts should provide access to technology and other supports that can make it easier for students to complete rigorous schoolwork at home.

If you live in a state or school district that is currently examining their homework policies, we suggest that you obtain a copy of the 2018 report from the Center for American Progress, as the report expands in great detail on each of the points we listed above.

Standardized Testing

Public schools have been administering standardized tests for generations. The Elementary and Secondary Education Act in 1965 opened the way for the increased use of norm-referenced tests to evaluate programs. In 2001, Congress passed No Child Left Behind, which expanded state-mandated standardized testing in math and reading as a means of assessing school performance. Most students from third grade through eighth grade, and again in high school, are tested annually unless a school has received permission to opt out. As a result, some public schools and many private schools today have opted out and do not administer standardized tests on a regular basis.

In our educational community today, there is an increasing emphasis and reliance on standardized tests to measure not only student performance but also that of teachers, principals, and other administrators. Children are often given standardized tests that are used by schools, districts, states, provinces, and national agencies to determine such things as special funding and other support services that have little to do with individual children. However, when these tests are used for the placement of students or for specialized instructional purposes, then they do impact your child very directly.

Our children are intimately involved in a sort of "high-stakes game" where they and others are being judged based on their performance at a given point in time rather than over a long period of time. This heavy reliance on standardized tests is questioned by many as being an inauthentic measure of actual performance and ability. While most parents firmly support higher academic standards, they oppose making important decisions about a child's future based on the results of a single test. It is far more important to recognize the reading and writing accomplishments of our children over a long period rather than at one random point in time.

Other measures such as teacher observations, student portfolios, and informal classroom tests are equally important and should be taken into account by the school. No child should be judged based solely on a test that spans an hour or two. As a parent, you need to be aware of how your child's school district makes decisions that will directly affect your child. Speak to your child's teacher and school principal about their philosophy of testing. If they rely solely on test data, then work within your parent association to have that modified. While standardized tests do provide valuable information, never forget that they are only one source of information.

As teachers and administrators are increasingly being judged by the performance of their students, this filters down to the children and often places undue pressure on them. In too many classrooms, we see situations such as the following:

> Teacher: "Okay, boys and girls, for the next few weeks, we are going to concentrate on getting ready for the reading and math tests. I hope you know how important these tests are to your future. These tests will help us determine if you have to go to summer school or if you can go on to the next grade. It is really important that you concentrate all your efforts and energies over the next few weeks to get ready for the tests."

This is often followed by daily barrages of worksheets and practice exercises similar to those that will be found on the exams. Is it any wonder our children feel stressed when it comes time to take the tests? As parents, we can help our children by putting the test situation in proper perspective and by helping our children to real-ize that their performance over time is what counts and what is really important.

As your child progresses through the grades in school, she will begin to encounter situations where there will be some pressure to perform in both reading and writing. Your job is to minimize this pressure on your child. Make sure that you and your child spend extra time during the "testing months" on fun activities. Encourage your child to engage in sports, as participation in physical activi-ties can often help to relieve stress. Take family walks and talk about anything other than school. But if you sense that your child is under pressure or feeling apprehensive, be sure to discuss these feelings with her. Share with your child stories of times when you were con-fronted with similar situations, whether as a student or as an adult. Share some of your coping strategies with your child, and encourage her to discuss her feelings with you.

Talk to your child's teacher if you perceive that he is placing too much pressure on your child. While it is important for students to learn how to take tests, such test practice activities should not per-vade the school day. Make sure, too, that you do not compound this situation by comparing your child with others or by giving in to your own anxiety about your child's performance. It's hard not to be anx-ious. We often think of our child's school performance as a direct reflection of our parenting, but that can be a dangerous situation for all concerned. Consider the case of a reading specialist we know who often spoke out against placing too much weight on such tests. He was a much sought-after speaker at local parent groups and professional education groups. He spoke of the need for authentic measures of student performance, decrying standardized tests as improper and flawed measures. Yet, much to his dismay, when his own daughter took her first "reading" test and scored a very high mark, he reportedly "heaved a sigh of relief," secure in the knowl-edge that "she's good in school."

By regularly providing encouragement and support in children's efforts and accomplishments, we can help them build internal strength and confidence. The section below is from the Whitby school and summarizes their position on standardized testing.

The pros:

- Standardized testing is a metric for learning.
- Standardized testing helps pinpoint areas for improvement.
- Standardized tests can help schools evaluate progress.

The cons:

- Test scores can impact confidence.
- There's pressure to "teach to the test."
- Scores don't provide a true picture of a student's ability.

Standardized testing is truthfully a very difficult issue because we do need internal and external assessments to measure student success. Assessments are useful when they're used as data to help schools improve the quality of the teaching and learning. They become harmful, however, when tests are used to judge students' natural abilities and when educators are put under pressure to teach to the test. Schools and parents should always look at standardized tests not as a value judgment but as an additional data point that can provide some perspective on student learning. (Whitby School, Diocese of Parramatta, Australia)

Personal Communication

Computers have become part of everyday life, both for us and for our children. While we have discussed the use of computers in chapters 3 through 6, we did not include any references to how the computer can be used for personal communication other than email. Beginning in our infancy and continuing into adulthood, computers can provide a path through which we can interact with others whom we are unable to see or hear in person. By using platforms such as Skype, FaceTime, Google Duo, and Zoom, we can have interactive conversations between groups of adults and/or children or just between two individuals having a video chat.

Research has shown that infants as young as eight months respond very well to interactions with other people, especially their grandparents, who can live some distance away. As long as the person on the other side of the screen is responding in real time, they are staying connected to each other. Make sure to use the same greeting and the same tone of voice with infants and toddlers to help them recognize you each time you have a video chat. Since a video chat only involves sight and sound, the young child needs to concentrate on those two senses. Before speech develops, infants recognize the family members they see and hear and like to show them their possessions, such as toys and books. These video chats seem to enhance even a very young child's language learning.

Parents who have technical expertise can even connect three families living in different parts of the world so that they can all interact with each other. This of course requires advance planning. One family we know sets aside a specific hour every Sunday night for a video chat. With older children, FaceTime is great and can be used on a portable device such as a phone, laptop, or tablet. Then they can walk around with it and show you things in the house, such as a project they are working on or a favorite book. They may even want to share a book by reading a page or two. One eight-year-old we know reads a bedtime story to his grandmother every night via FaceTime.

Skype and Google Duo can both be downloaded without any charge on any computer, mobile phone, or tablet and used in the same way as FaceTime, with similar results. All of the video chats on these platforms can be made more interactive with some advance planning. For example, two individuals can have the same piece of chocolate candy and pretend to share it by handing it to each other via the camera.

Zoom, which began as a business platform to connect personnel who were not in the same location but needed to confer with each other, has now been adapted for use in more social situations. Birthday parties for both adults and children of all ages have become popular. Zoom does require a host who arranges for the time, invites participants, and arranges for a link that allows each participant to join the group. It is very interactive, as everyone in the group can comment, raise questions, and respond to others. At present, Zoom is a free platform, but it does have a time limit for each event, which may be extended by paying a fee.

If Your Child Needs Help

The fact that your child has a reading or writing problem may not be obvious to you, particularly in the early years when children are just learning to read. For many children, learning to read occurs with such ease that it seems a simple task; for others, it requires a more concentrated effort; and for a small number, learning to read is a truly difficult task. If we bear in mind that children progress at different rates, particularly in the early school years, what may seem like a learning problem at the start of elementary school may simply be a different rate of progress, rendering intervention unnecessary. Sometimes the first clue you have as a parent that your child is having a problem is a word from his teacher in the form of a note to make an appointment for a parent-teacher conference, or possibly a notation on a report sent home. On the other hand, as the parent, you may become aware of some learning problem before you have any contact with your child's teacher. In either case, once you know that your child is having some difficulty, the most important first step is to talk to the teacher.

An in-person conference with your child's teacher may result in her suggesting several options, including some specific things that you can do with your child. The first option you have is to see if your child's school offers special help in reading and writing. If this is the case, then the classroom teacher will arrange for your child to see a reading teacher or literacy specialist. In many schools today, there is a teacher who is specifically licensed to work with children who are having learning problems and who is in the best position to diagnose your child's difficulties and to plan a program of intervention. In general, your child will work with a reading specialist either in a small group or sometimes even on a one-to-one basis several times a week. This extra instruction may take place in the regular classroom or in an alternative setting. The classroom teacher and the reading specialist work together to ensure that there is appropriate progress and that the regular classroom instruction is integrated with the work of the specialist. It is critical to remember that no one program works for all children and that it is the reading specialist who will best know your child's needs. Most reading specialists use an approach combining many methods, and they continually assess progress to see if what they are doing is working for an individual child.

If there are no special services available within the school, there are still several other options available to you. For instance, your child's teacher can continue to be a valuable resource by referring you to a specific tutor known to her who will work with your child on a one-to-one basis. The most important considerations here are the tutor's qualifications and experience and recommendations from other parents, as well as references from the tutor's previous clients. Regardless of how you select a tutor, it's essential that there be an interview, at which time you can observe the tutor's interaction with your child. It's also important to know what specific methods the tutor is planning to use so that there's no conflict with what is happening at school. A tutor ideally should meet with your child's teacher to ensure that they are working cooperatively and not at cross-purposes.

Another possible option, if you happen to live in the vicinity of a college or university that offers teacher preparation, is that they have a clinic or center where they work with children who are having learning problems. Generally this means that college students who are taking coursework in how to teach reading will tutor children who live in the surrounding area as part of their college program. In much the same way as a reading specialist works, they will diagnose your child's strengths and weaknesses and plan a program of instruction. Although your child is being tutored by students, the students will be working under the supervision of their college professor. In this setting, the parent is kept informed of a child's progress and is encouraged to meet with the tutor, who will frequently offer suggestions for helping the child at home.

Finally, it is essential that your child is in general good health. A child who is in poor general health or who suffers from chronic illness is frequently unable to pay appropriate attention in school and may tire easily during the school day, making concentrating on tasks that involve reading and writing difficult. Also, chronic illness may result in excessive absence from school. A loss of instruction at crucial times, particularly in the early years, when learning to read is such an important part of the school day, may result in reading problems later on. So much of learning involves listening, and seeing that, it is critical to make sure that your child's eyes and ears function properly. Nothing is more frustrating to a child than being unable to hear the teacher and classmates or being unable to see the chalkboard clearly.

Observing your child at home can give you important information about any hearing or vision problems. You may become aware of a hearing problem if you notice that your child does not seem to respond to your voice or is unaware of loud sounds in the house or the street. A vision problem can be spotted if your child complains of burning or itching eyes, has frequent headaches, squints noticeably at near or far objects, seems to hold books or papers very close to his eyes, or mentions that words in his books are blurred. Your child is an important source of information. Simply asking him what is bothering him either in school or at home can yield some surprising answers, particularly in the areas of vision and hearing. Both hearing and vision problems require the services of a professional and should be taken care of as soon as they become obvious.

As a parent who is concerned about your child's difficulties in school, you can do several things in addition to the options discussed above. As an example, it's always easier to read material when you are familiar with the topic and some of the words. Your child will encounter more difficulty when she needs to read stories and other material about unfamiliar people, animals, and places, and as a result, she may become thoroughly frustrated. Therefore, the more experiences that you can provide that are in some way related to what is being taught in school, the more successful your child will be in classroom activities. One way to find out what topics will be studied in a particular year is simply to write a note to the teacher requesting that information and indicating that you are planning some trips and, if possible, would like to coordinate the classroom work with your plans.

For example, if one of the science topics this year is the earth and the planets, then planning a visit to a planetarium will prove extremely worthwhile. Words and concepts such as *orbit, moon, stars, sun, nova,* and *black hole* will all become more meaningful and as a result will be better understood when your child meets them in a book. Similarly, in the early school years, there's often a focus on animals, so a visit to the local zoo, where you can read the signs together as you view the animals, can be great fun. Many zoos house animals such as rhinos, elephants, zebras, and giraffes from the same part of the world together, and since they come from Africa, here's an opportunity to locate Africa on a map. In addition, buying a book at the zoo shop on African animals or looking for one in your local library will greatly add to your child's knowledge of this topic. Other topics that are included in the early grades are learning about families, food, and work. You can help to expand your child's vocabulary by using words such as *brother, sister, twins, siblings, aunt, uncle, grandparents, cousins,* and *parent* when talking about the family or when visiting relatives.

Also, most children are interested in the world of work, so visiting places where family members work and using language related to the job will extend a child's knowledge and language. Should an opportunity arise to visit a local newspaper, then terms such as *newsprint, computer, reporter, editor, advertisements, sports depart-ment, local news, national news, international news,* and *obituaries* will take on added meaning. Other possibilities include visiting lo-cal businesses, such as food stores, banks, shops, or cleaners, and service agencies, such as the post office and fire, police, or highway departments. The people working in these places frequently use specialized vocabulary, and when your child hears the words within a "real setting" as opposed to simply in a book, they take on a special meaning. Then, when he sees these words later in a book, he'll asso-ciate them with his experience and find it easier to understand and remember them.

Another idea is to discuss things he wants to know in advance of a trip. You could then jot down some of his questions, reading them together after you write them. As a follow-up, you could read the questions again after the trip to see which ones were answered and which ones still need answers. You could suggest looking on the internet, going to the library, or asking a knowledgeable individual, but only if your child shows real interest. Another possibility is writ-ing something about the trip. A beginning reader who is having diffi-culty learning to read can dictate the sentences while you write them down. Older readers who need some help can write independently and then with your help reread what they have written. Children can then either draw a picture, add a photo if they used a camera, or cut out a picture from a magazine to go with the story.

Reading the mail, advertisements, emails, and letters can all be a part of the day's activities. While we tend to think of "reading to-gether" as meaning that you and your child are sitting together, in fact, this need not necessarily be the case. For example, you might be preparing dinner while your child looks through the day's mail and tells you about it. This doesn't mean that he needs to be able to read all the words—just enough to get a sense of what is there. Are there advertisements from local stores? Are there bills? Is there a personal letter or card? Another opportunity is when you are both in the car. Asking your child to read street signs, billboards, car makes and license plates, and storefront ads are all excellent opportunities to focus on words and their meanings.

While we have stressed the importance of reading aloud to children of all developmental levels, for the reader who is having difficulty with reading, this becomes a daunting activity. It may involve a slightly different approach than reading aloud to a young child, which we discussed in detail in chapter 3. The vocabulary you use and the conversation that the two of you engage in, both during the listening time and at the end of the selection, will be very different, but the process is basically the same. You may want to reread chapter 3, Your Preschool Child, to see an example of reading aloud to a three- to five-year-old and adapt the process to the age of your child as you share reading and listening with him.

Of course, not all children who are having problems in reading are able to talk about what is bothering them. It's your responsibility as the parent to be on the lookout for potential problems and if you suspect them to bring them to the attention of the school. Likewise, it's the responsibility of the classroom teacher and other school personnel to keep you informed of any problems that they may have spotted. Test anxiety can certainly be a problem, particularly for a child who is not a proficient reader. This situation requires open communication between you and the classroom teacher, who may recommend some effective and successful solutions for dealing with mandated standardized testing. It is parents and teachers working together as a team who provide the most effective help for children who are having difficulties in learning.

Many of the activities that we described for the young reader, the evolving reader, and the maturing reader are appropriate for a child who is having difficulties with reading and writing. As we have stressed before, the key is to know your child, his strengths as well as his limitations, and to select those activities that are appropriate to your child's reading and writing abilities. Follow his lead in selecting an activity that is of high interest and that will be fun for both of you, but then be ready to stop anytime if he is bored or inattentive. The key to progress in reading is to read more, and your child will only do that if reading becomes an enjoyable activity.

This chapter, which may be read at any time, has focused only on the four topics that we think cut across all developmental levels and children of all ages. We hope you have found the information useful and are able to adapt it to the needs of your family and child.

Afterword

In this book, we have shared our decades of experience as teachers, researchers, and parents to give you an overview of how children develop their reading and writing abilities from birth through early adolescence on their road to becoming proficient readers and writers. Parents and caregivers, along with teachers, are in the best position to provide activities that will further develop children's learning. We are aware that we all live in a busy world and are frequently overworked and overwhelmed with our many activities. Above all, we do not want to add to that stress. Our mindset in writing this book was that in describing many everyday events, we could help you greatly enhance children's literacy abilities. We hope you have tried some of the examples we have provided and that you have found this book to be informative and readable.

As writers, we hope you read the book in its entirety, but we also want to encourage you to reread those chapters that pertain to the developmental level most appropriate to the child in your care. Since children develop at different levels, it is important that you reread the chapter that most closely fits your child. For example, chapter 5, Evolving Readers and Writers, may be a better fit for your child than chapter 4, Young Readers and Writers. You are the best judge of your child's level of reading and writing abilities. It is important for you to select activities that may be in a different chapter if you think they would be of interest to and fun for both of you.

Finally, we hope to learn more about how children learn. We are interested in knowing who you are and what you found most informative and useful in this book. We are especially interested in your comments about the activities you and your child enjoyed the most, as well as those that appeared to both of you to be less helpful. Please email your comments to RaisingReadersandWriters2020@gmail.com, and we will be pleased to respond.

Read Together!
Write Together!

Acknowledgments

Many people helped us as we began to construct the contents of our book. First we want to thank the parents who responded to the questionnaire that we sent out to gather information about their children's reading and writing. Their comments enabled us to plan the content of the book and focus our writing on the common areas of greatest concern. Our perspectives were further enhanced by our New York University graduate students who shared their real-life and teaching experiences with us over many years.

We were assisted in the final production of this book by the expertise and thoughtful comments from our Elite Authors editorial team; Sarah Lange Davis, Heather Wallace, Lydia Bowman, Lara. and Talia.

Special words of thanks go to our children, Jill, Greg, Heidi, Rob, Adam and Allison for sharing their lives with us and giving us many insights into how they learned to read and write as they moved from infancy to adulthood. An extra special thanks to our grandchildren, Ben, Adam, Evan, and Max, for allowing us to interact with them as they moved through the various phases of their development. We are so pleased to see them grow into mature readers and writers.

Finally, we want to acknowledge our husbands. I, Carole, will forever be indebted to my husband, Barry Rhodes, who mostly did not complain as he edited my writing throughout our many years together. He taught me everything I know about writing and still sits on my shoulder as I continue to write. Harvey Nadler, Lenore's husband, is a wonderful listener and was always supportive and understanding of her time away from him as we wrote this book. As a linguist, Harvey was amused at Lenore's grammatical missteps and served as a great editor for both of us.

Carole and Lenore

Made in the USA
Middletown, DE
01 May 2021

38179239R00099